George Foreman®
THE NEXT
GRILLERATION™
GREAT GRILLING RECIPES

Written by George Foreman
& Connie Merydith

Pascoe Publishing, Inc.
Rocklin, California

00-102216

ISBN: 1-929862-46-6

05   06   07   08   10   9   8   7   6   5   4   3   2   1

Printed in China

Table of Contents

PREFACE

Dear Friends,

Many of you know me as the heavyweight boxing champion of the world, but very few of you probably know that eating the right kinds of food helped create the foundation for my success and that this remains a key part of my life today.

My story really begins when I was very young. You see, as a kid growing up in Houston, my family didn't always have enough to eat. My mother worked every day of the week to provide for the seven children in our family, but money was scarce and sometimes we were all hungry. I grew up quickly and my appetite was rarely satisfied. My mother could hardly keep up with my constant search for food! But, my mother was very smart and creative in the meals she prepared for us. She would add a small amount of meat to a large amount of vegetables for a main meal. Or, she would dish up vegetables and rice or pasta and leave out the meat altogether. At the time, we didn't realize that we were actually eating a diet that was good for us, we only knew that meat, fish, poultry and specialty foods were pure luxury items. I would save my money whenever I could, a nickel at a time, and use it to buy a big cheeseburger or some other special treat. I was constantly thinking about food! Because of this, you can probably imagine how much I loved steaks, chops, ribs and all the trimmings when I became an adult!

During my boxing career in the 1960s, I was in great physical shape and regularly ate hefty steaks and large green salads as part of my training program. I was a healthy six-foot, four-inch tall boxer and I weighed in around 230 pounds. In those days, when I was hungry—I was really hungry! My career as a professional boxer quickly gained momentum and in 1968 I won the heavyweight gold medal for boxing at the Olympics. During the next several years, I ate everything I wanted, as often as I wanted, and by the time I reached the ultimate status of heavyweight champion of the world, I had a heavyweight appetite to match my heavyweight title.

In 1986, after ten years of retirement from the ring, I sat back and took a hard look at myself. I weighed in at over 300 pounds and was completely out of shape. My diet for the past several years had been whatever I wanted it to be: pizza, fried chicken, ice cream and many fast-food favorites. At the time, I didn't give much thought to the damage those foods were doing to my body. After all, I was retired, right? Wrong. I decided to go back into the boxing ring once again.

To prepare for my introduction back into boxing, I had to look at the types of food I was eating. I was eating large amounts of protein, but not as many carbohydrates as I needed for energy. I was eating a diet very high in fat and I wasn't getting the exercise my body needed for good health. So, I began to run again. I worked on regaining my strength and form. I cut most of the red meat from my diet and concentrated on fish, poultry, complex carbohydrates and other foods that would build up my strength while eliminating the fat. And, when I re-entered the ring in 1987, I was in excellent physical shape and I knew that, once again, I was ready to become a champion.

Today I still enjoy delicious food and I eat with a hearty appetite. But, I choose foods carefully and I watch the amount of fat that I eat. I keep my diet balanced and I exercise regularly to keep myself in good shape. The recipes in this cookbook were created by Connie and me to help you accomplish exactly the same goals. Inside these chapters you'll find a wide variety of recipes for healthful grilled foods that cut out fat, not the flavor. Each recipe has been analyzed for fat, calories and other important nutritional information. But, just as importantly, these recipes have been created to taste really good. Try some of our favorites, such as *Orange Pressed Tuna, Jerk Chicken with Cilantro Rice, Creamy Dill Carrots* and *Quick & Easy Grilled Bananas.* A true champion succeeds in reaching the goal he or she desires, whatever that goal may be. We believe that the recipes in this cookbook and *The George Foreman® Lean Mean Fat Reducing Grilling Machine* can be part of your own success story. Enjoy!

George Foreman

INTRODUCTION

Welcome to The Next Grilleration™. Your *George Foreman® Lean Mean Fat Reducing Grilling Machine*—made popular by millions of people who love delicious grilled steaks, chops, burgers and more—is now better than ever!

Over the past several years, people everywhere have used *The George Foreman® Lean Mean Fat Reducing Grilling Machine* because it is quick, easy and grills everything they love to eat. Ask students, young adults, career executives, families and retirees what foods they grill and you will hear a wide array of creative answers—French fries, croissant sandwiches, salmon fillets, frozen pizza pockets and even fresh fruit! Everyone has a favorite food for their own "George" grill. Introduced as the perfect grilling machine for steaks and hamburgers, *The George Foreman® Lean Mean Fat Reducing Grilling Machine* has actually become much, much more for millions of busy people.

Now, with the added convenience of the variable temperature control, the electronic timer for precise grilling and the removable grilling plates for easy clean-up, you have entered the Next Grilleration™ with *The George Foreman® Lean Mean Fat Reducing Grilling Machine*!

Your *George Foreman® Lean Mean Fat Reducing Grilling Machine* allows fat to drip away from foods as they grill, resulting in tender, flavorful foods without the heavy fat. The recipes inside this book were created specifically for *The George Foreman® Lean Mean Fat Reducing Grilling Machine* and each has been designed to help you maintain a healthy lifestyle.

Try the *Grilled Asian Beef*, *Caribbean Jerk Pork*, *Lemon Basil Halibut* and *Pineapple Honey Chicken Breasts* for excellent entrées. Add *Dijon Parsley Potatoes*, *Zesty Marinated Zucchini*, or *Rosemary & Sage Potatoes* to your grilled chops or steaks. And, for outstanding desserts, choose *Grilled Apple Pecan Cups* or *Hawaiian Pineapple Slices*. Almost all of our recipes are low in fat and sodium and, if you are following a high-protein, low-carbohydrate diet, you'll find recipes tagged with a special "LOW CARB" icon. Each recipe also includes a nutritional analysis so that you can make healthful meal choices.

Welcome to the world of delicious grilling with *The George Foreman® Lean Mean Fat Reducing Grilling Machine*—welcome to the Next Grilleration™!

GRILLING TIPS
— Get the Basics

TIP 1

The first thing you should know about your *George Foreman®
Lean Mean Fat Reducing Grilling Machine* is that it is
designed to channel fat away from foods as they grill. You'll
notice this design as soon as you open the grill. Foods won't
sit in fat as they grill and foods won't absorb fat as they grill.
Less fat is a good thing.

The removable grilling plates of *The George Foreman® Lean
Mean Fat Reducing Grilling Machine* have a special nonstick
coating, which means that you don't need to mess around
with oil or butter before grilling. You may want to lightly coat
the grilling plates with nonstick cooking spray if you are going
to grill foods that can stick to the plates, such as foods
coated with honey or sugar.

TIP 2

TIP 3

The George Foreman® Lean Mean Fat Reducing Grilling Machine has a variable temperature control and an electronic timer to grill foods to perfection. Set the Temperature and Timer as directed in each recipe or use the Basic Cooking Guide in the back of this book as a general guideline when preparing foods. Remember that your foods may grill more quickly or slowly than indicated due to the thickness of the food or other variables.

The heating elements in *The George Foreman® Lean Mean Fat Reducing Grilling Machine* cook both sides of your food at once for fast and even grilling. You don't need to turn the food—set the Temperature and the Timer and relax.

TIP 4

TIP 5

Follow the manufacturer's instructions carefully when using the drip trays, spatulas and other grilling accessories. Use only heat-tolerant plastic spatulas on the nonstick grilling plates.

When grilling meat, carefully check for "doneness" by inserting the tip of a sharp knife into the meat. Do not cut through the meat or touch the grill with the knife. Use caution when opening the heated grill.

Children may enjoy assisting with food preparation, however they should not touch or use the grill while it is hot. They should not stand near the grill or sit on the kitchen counter as it operates.

TIP 7

Follow the manufacturer's instructions for safely cleaning your grill. Clean the grill housing properly each time you use it and don't use harsh cleansers or steel scouring pads. Remove the grilling plates as directed and wash in warm water with a mild dish detergent. If you want to loosen any foods, use the plastic spatula or a soft cloth. Dry the plates and place them in the grill. It's that easy.

BRING OUT THE BEST OF GRILLING
—Marinades, Sauces & Rubs

Beef, poultry, pork and fish each have distinctively different flavors and textures. Grilling adds personality to each of these choices, however the addition of a marinade, sauce or rub can make the difference between a standard meal and a truly memorable one. We don't believe that eating in a healthy way needs to be a boring experience, so we created the following recipes to put a little zip, a bit of a bite and a tiny bit of tanginess into your meals.

Each of these recipes can be made ahead of time and stored, depending on the ingredients in them. Marinades are especially useful when grilling lean cuts of meat because they help break down connective tissue in the meat. Use the marinades when you want to plan ahead for tomorrow or for a casual dinner party with friends. To save time, you can prepare marinades in a large, self-sealing plastic bag and place the meat in it. Close the bag tightly and refrigerate for several hours. When you are ready to grill, simply throw the bag and marinade away. Don't re-use a marinade as a table sauce unless you boil it for at least 5 minutes first to remove any bacteria.

Try the sauces for a change of pace when you're ready to explore new flavors. Sauces add interest to what can otherwise be a fairly basic cut of poultry or meat. Many sauces are cooked first and used as an accompaniment at the table. To use sauces in your *George Foreman® Lean Mean Fat Reducing Grilling Machine,* you can either pour one spoonful of sauce over each piece of meat, reserving the rest for the table, or you can completely cover the meat with sauce. If you choose to cover the meat completely with a sauce, the sauce will melt and run into the drip tray. Empty the drip tray as needed.

Use rubs when you want to prepare a quick and easy entrée that offers a bold taste. Rubs are a spicy combination of flavors that perk up meat, poultry and fish in a second. As a timesaver, you can mix and store any of these rubs in a self-sealing plastic bag. When you are ready to grill, put the meat into the bag and shake to cover the meat with the spices. Clean up is quick and easy—discard the bag and grill the meat. You may also add a rub to the meat by putting the spice mixture on a plate and pressing the meat into it.

After you've tried these recipes, we hope that you will experiment with some of your own. Add marinades, sauces and rubs to make the most of meat, seafood and poultry in your *George Foreman® Lean Mean Fat Reducing Grilling Machine.*

MARINADES
Spicy Orange Marinade

Marinates chicken breasts or pork with tangy flavor.

1/2 c./120 ml.	orange juice
1/2 t./2.5 g.	orange zest, finely grated
1 t./5 ml.	Dijon mustard
2 T./30 ml.	cider vinegar
2 T./28 g.	dark or light brown sugar
2 T./30 ml.	extra virgin olive oil
1	clove garlic, finely chopped

Combine all ingredients in a small saucepan and simmer 3 minutes over low heat. Use immediately or store in an airtight container in the refrigerator for up to 1 week.

MAKES ABOUT 3/4 CUP/210 ML.

NUTRITIONAL ANALYSIS: Calories: **25**   Total fat: **2g**   Saturated fat: **>1g**
% calories from fat: **64**   Carbohydrates: **2 g**   Protein: **0 g**   Cholesterol: **0 mg**   Sodium: **9 mg**

LOW CARB

Easy Italian Marinade

Fast and easy to prepare, this marinade produces a wonderful flavor when paired with beef, pork or poultry.

1/3 c./80 ml.	extra virgin olive oil
2 T./30 ml.	balsamic vinegar
1 t./5 g.	fresh basil, finely chopped
1	clove garlic, minced
1/2 t./2.5 g.	black pepper
1 t./5 g.	dry mustard
1/4 t./1 g.	salt

Mix all ingredients in a small bowl and pour over beef, chicken or pork. Store any unused marinade in an airtight container in the refrigerator for up to 2 weeks.

MAKES ABOUT 1/3 CUP/80 ML.

NUTRITIONAL ANALYSIS: Calories: **14**   Total fat: **0g**   Saturated fat: **0g**
% calories from fat: **0**   Carbohydrates: **3 g**   Protein: **>1 g**   Cholesterol: **0 mg**   Sodium: **169 mg**

Beefy Pepper Marinade

The pepper in this marinade makes the difference!

2 T./30 ml.	extra virgin olive oil
1/4 c./60 ml.	white vinegar
1/2 c./120 ml.	lemon juice
2 T./28 g.	honey
2 t./10 g.	black pepper
2	cloves garlic, finely minced

Mix all ingredients in a small bowl to completely dissolve the honey. Use as a marinade for beef or lamb. Store any unused marinade in an airtight container in the refrigerator for up to 1 week.

MAKES 3/4 CUP/210 ML.

NUTRITIONAL ANALYSIS: Calories: **8**   Total fat: **1g**   Saturated fat: **1g**
% calories from fat: **22**   Carbohydrates: **3 g**   Protein: **>1 g**   Cholesterol: **0 mg**   Sodium: **>1 mg**

Tangy Pork Marinade

A robust marinade perfect for pork.

2 T./30 ml.	extra virgin olive oil
1/4 c./55 g.	fresh parsley, finely chopped
2	cloves garlic, finely minced
1/2 t./2.5 g.	black pepper
1/4 t./1 g.	cayenne pepper
1/2 c./120 ml.	Worcestershire sauce
1/4 c./60 ml.	low sodium soy sauce
1/4 c./60 ml.	balsamic vinegar

Combine all ingredients in a small bowl. Store any unused marinade in an airtight container in the refrigerator for up to 1 week.

MAKES ABOUT 1 1/2 CUPS/350 ML.

LOW CARB

NUTRITIONAL ANALYSIS: Calories: **18** Total fat: **1g** Saturated fat: **>1g**
% calories from fat: **58** Carbohydrates: **2 g** Protein: **>1 g** Cholesterol: **0 mg** Sodium: **388 mg**

Lemon & Herb Marinade

A light and flavorful marinade.

1 c./250 ml.	lemon juice
2 T./30 ml.	extra virgin olive oil
1/3 c./80 ml.	red wine vinegar
1 t./5 g.	fresh oregano, minced
1 t./5 g.	fresh thyme, minced
1 t./5 g.	black pepper
1/2 t./2.5 g.	salt
1	clove garlic, finely chopped

Mix all ingredients in a small bowl. Store any unused marinade in an airtight container in the refrigerator for up to 2 weeks.

MAKES ABOUT 1 1/2 CUPS/350 ML.

NUTRITIONAL ANALYSIS: Calories: **13** Total fat: **1g** Saturated fat: **>1g**
% calories from fat: **69** Carbohydrates: **>1 g** Protein: **>1 g** Cholesterol: **0 mg** Sodium: **45 mg**

Zesty Beef Marinade

Bold flavors combine for a delightful change!

1/2 c./120 ml.	**fresh lemon juice**
1/2 c./120 ml.	**balsamic vinegar**
1/2 c./120 ml.	**low sodium soy sauce**
2 T./30 ml.	**vegetable oil**
1/4 c./60 ml.	**Worcestershire sauce**
3 T./42 g.	**fresh parsley, finely minced**
3	**cloves garlic, finely minced**
1 T./14 g.	**black pepper**
1 t./5 g.	**salt**
2 T./30 ml.	**Dijon mustard**

Thoroughly whisk all ingredients in a small bowl. Store any unused marinade in an airtight container in the refrigerator for up to 1 week.

MAKES ABOUT 2 1/2 CUPS/600 ML.

LOW CARB

NUTRITIONAL   ANALYSIS: Calories: **14**   Total fat: **>1g**   Saturated fat: **>1g**
% calories from fat: **48**   Carbohydrates: **2 g**   Protein: **>1 g**   Cholesterol: **0 mg**   Sodium: **313 mg**

Herb Mustard Marinade

Classic partners for pork or lamb.

1/2 c./120 ml.	Dijon mustard
1/4 c./60 ml.	water
2 T./30 ml.	extra virgin olive oil
1 t./5 g.	dried thyme
1 t./5 g.	dried sage
1 t./5 g.	dried rosemary
1	clove garlic, finely minced

Mix all ingredients in a small bowl. Store any unused marinade in an airtight container in the refrigerator for up to 1 week.

MAKES ABOUT 1/2 CUP/120 ML.

NUTRITIONAL ANALYSIS: Calories: **26**   Total fat: **2g**   Saturated fat: **>1g**
% calories from fat: **77**   Carbohydrates: **1 g**   Protein: **>1 g**   Cholesterol: **0 mg**   Sodium: **195 mg**

East Indian Marinade

Fresh ingredients and flavors make this marinade really special.
Try this with beef, lamb or chicken.

1 t./5 g.	fresh mint, finely chopped
1/4 t./1 g.	salt
1 t./5 g.	black pepper
1/4 c./55 g.	yellow/strong onion, finely chopped
1 T./14 g.	fresh parsley, finely chopped
2	cloves garlic, finely minced
8 oz./235 ml.	unflavored, lowfat yogurt
1/2 c./115 g.	cucumber, chopped
1/2 c./115 g.	red tomatoes, chopped

Combine all ingredients in a small bowl. Use immediately.

MAKES ABOUT 2 CUPS/550 ML.

NUTRITIONAL ANALYSIS: Calories: **7** Total fat: **>1g** Saturated fat: **>1g**
% calories from fat: **18** Carbohydrates: **>1 g** Protein: **>1 g** Cholesterol: **>1 mg** Sodium: **24 mg**

Spicy Oriental Marinade

Five-spice powder can be found in the specialty food aisle of your grocery store.

2 T./30 ml.	**peanut oil**
1 T./14 g.	**ground ginger**
1 T./14 g.	**five-spice powder**
1 T./14 g.	**cayenne pepper**
1/2 c./115 g.	**green/spring onions, finely chopped**
1/2 c./120 ml.	**low sodium soy sauce**
1/4 c./60 ml.	**red wine vinegar**

Mix all ingredients in a small bowl. Store any unused marinade in an airtight container in the refrigerator for up to 1 week.

MAKES 1 1/2 CUPS/350 ML.

NUTRITIONAL ANALYSIS: Calories: **17**   Total fat: **1g**   Saturated fat: **>1g**
% calories from fat: **64**   Carbohydrates: **1 g**   Protein: **>1 g**   Cholesterol: **0 mg**   Sodium: **374 mg**

Greek Island Marinade

Exotic flavor for chicken or lamb!

1/4 c./60 ml.	lemon juice
8 oz./235 ml.	unflavored, lowfat yogurt
1/2 c./115 g.	fresh mint, finely chopped
1/4 c./55 g.	fresh parsley, finely chopped
1/4 c./55 g.	yellow/strong onion, finely chopped
1/2 t./2.5 g.	cayenne pepper
1/2 t./2.5 g.	black pepper
1/4 t./1 g.	ground cinnamon

Combine all ingredients in a small bowl. Use immediately.

MAKES ABOUT 2 1/2 CUPS/600 ML.

NUTRITIONAL ANALYSIS: Calories: **6**   Total fat: **>1g**   Saturated fat: **>1g**   % calories from fat: **18**   Carbohydrates: **1 g**   Protein: **>1 g**   Cholesterol: **>1 mg**   Sodium: **7 mg**

Barbeque Chicken Marinade

This marinade creates a mouth-watering, rich flavor for chicken or turkey.

1 T./15 ml.	extra virgin olive oil
2 t./10 g.	salt
6 oz./170 g.	can tomato paste
1 c./250 ml.	cider vinegar
2 T./28 g.	sugar
1 T./14 g.	cayenne pepper
1 c./250 ml.	nonfat chicken broth/stock
2 T./30 ml.	Worcestershire sauce

Whisk all ingredients together in a small saucepan and simmer gently for 5 minutes. Refrigerate to cool completely before use. Store in the refrigerator for up to 2 weeks.

MAKES ABOUT 2 1/2 CUPS/600 ML.

NUTRITIONAL ANALYSIS: Calories: **9**   Total fat: **>1g**   Saturated fat: **>1g**
% calories from fat: **27**   Carbohydrates: **2 g**   Protein: **>1 g**   Cholesterol: **0 mg**   Sodium: **123 mg**

Gina's Teriyaki Marinade

Partner with beef flank/skirt steak.

1/4 c./60 ml.	**vegetable oil**
1/2 c./120 ml.	**low sodium soy sauce**
1/4 c./55 g.	**honey**
2 T./30 ml.	**vinegar**
2 T./28 g.	**green/spring onions, finely chopped**
1 1/2 t./7 g.	**ground ginger**
1	**clove garlic, finely minced**

Combine all ingredients in a small bowl. Store any unused marinade in an airtight container in the refrigerator for up to 1 week.

MAKES ABOUT 1 CUP/250 ML.

LOW CARB

NUTRITIONAL ANALYSIS: Calories: **35**   Total fat: **2g**   Saturated fat: **>1g**
% calories from fat: **56**   Carbohydrates: **4 g**   Protein: **>1 g**   Cholesterol: **0 mg**   Sodium: **348 mg**

Dill Marinade

A mild marinade with soft flavors that complements fish especially well.

1/4 c./55 g.	**fresh dill, finely minced**
1	**clove garlic, finely minced**
8 oz./235 ml.	**unflavored, lowfat yogurt**
2 T./30 ml.	**Dijon mustard**
2 T./30 ml.	**low sodium soy sauce**
1 T./15 ml.	**fresh lemon juice**

Mix all ingredients in a small bowl. Use immediately as a marinade for any firm fish.

MAKES ABOUT 1 1/2 CUPS/350 ML.

NUTRITIONAL ANALYSIS: Calories: **9** Total fat: **>1g** Saturated fat: **>1g**
% calories from fat: **26** Carbohydrates: **1 g** Protein: **>1 g** Cholesterol: **>1 mg** Sodium: **126 mg**

Hot & Spicy Asian Marinade

Asian chile oil and cayenne pepper combine to pack a punch!

2 T./30 ml.	**Asian chile oil**
1/2 t./2.5 g.	**cayenne pepper**
1/2 c./115 g.	**dark brown sugar**
1 t./5 g.	**ground ginger**
1 c./250 ml.	**low sodium soy sauce**
1/2 c./120 ml.	**water**
1/2 c./120 ml.	**white vinegar**
2	**cloves garlic, finely minced**

Combine all ingredients in a small bowl. Store any unused marinade in an airtight container in the refrigerator for up to 1 week.

MAKES ABOUT 2 1/2 CUPS/600 ML.

NUTRITIONAL ANALYSIS: Calories: **15**   Total fat: **>1g**   Saturated fat: **>1g**
% calories from fat: **36**   Carbohydrates: **2 g**   Protein: **>1 g**   Cholesterol: **0 mg**   Sodium: **346 mg**

SAUCES
All American Barbeque Sauce

Everyone's favorite for chicken, ribs, steak and more.

8 oz./235 ml.	prepared tomato sauce
1	small yellow/strong onion, chopped
3	cloves garlic, finely minced
1 T./14 g.	fresh parsley, finely minced
1 t./5 g.	black pepper
1/2 t./2.5 g.	cayenne pepper
1/2 t./2.5 g.	salt
1/4 c./60 ml.	cider vinegar
1 t./5 g.	dry yellow mustard

Combine all ingredients in a small saucepan and simmer over low heat for 8–10 minutes. Cool. Use immediately or store in an airtight container in the refrigerator for up to 2 weeks.

MAKES ABOUT 1 1/2 CUPS/350 ML.

NUTRITIONAL ANALYSIS: Calories: **6**   Total fat: **>1g**   Saturated fat: **0g**
% calories from fat: **6**   Carbohydrates: **1 g**   Protein: **>1 g**   Cholesterol: **0 mg**   Sodium: **66 mg**

LOW CARB

Beef Rib Sauce

Use as a marinade or dipping sauce for ribs.

4	**cloves garlic, finely minced**
1/4 c./55 g.	**white onion, finely chopped**
1/4 c./60 ml.	**ketchup**
1/4 c./60 ml.	**prepared yellow mustard**
1/4 c./60 ml.	**cider vinegar**
1/4 c./60 ml.	**water**
1/4 c./55 g.	**honey**
1 T./15 ml.	**extra virgin olive oil**
1 t./5 g.	**cayenne pepper**

Combine ingredients in a small saucepan. Stir and heat for 5 minutes. Cool. Use immediately or store in an airtight container in the refrigerator for up to 2 weeks. May be frozen, if desired.

MAKES ABOUT 1 1/2 CUPS/350 ML.

NUTRITIONAL ANALYSIS: Calories: **19**   Total fat: **>1g**   Saturated fat: **>1g**   % calories from fat: **26**   Carbohydrates: **4 g**   Protein: **>1 g**   Cholesterol: **0 mg**   Sodium: **54 mg**

East West Sauce

East (turmeric and ginger) meets West (ketchup and mustard).
You will find ground turmeric in the spice section of your grocery store.

1/4 c./60 ml.	low sodium soy sauce
1/2 c./115 g.	honey
1/2 c./120 ml.	ketchup
1 T./15 ml.	prepared yellow mustard
1 t./5 g.	garlic powder
1/2 t./2.5 g.	black pepper
1/2 t./2.5 g.	ground turmeric
1 t./5 g.	ground ginger
1 t./5 g.	salt

Mix all ingredients in a small saucepan. Simmer over low heat for 5 minutes. Use immediately or store in an airtight container in the refrigerator for up to 2 weeks.

MAKES ABOUT 1 1/2 CUPS/350 ML.

NUTRITIONAL ANALYSIS: Calories: **26** Total fat: **>1g** Saturated fat: **>1g**
% calories from fat: **2** Carbohydrates: **7 g** Protein: **>1 g** Cholesterol: **0 mg** Sodium: **289 mg**

LOW CARB

Southern Barbeque Sauce

For ribs, chops, steaks and more.

1/2 c./115 g.	dark brown sugar
2 c./475 ml.	tomato sauce
1/4 c./60 ml.	cider vinegar
2 T./30 ml.	prepared yellow mustard
1 t./5 g.	cayenne pepper
1 t./5 g.	black pepper
2 T./30 ml.	Worcestershire sauce
1/4 t./1 g.	ground paprika
1	clove garlic, finely minced
1/2	yellow/strong onion, finely chopped

Mix all ingredients thoroughly. Simmer in a medium saucepan over low heat for 10 minutes. Cool. Use immediately or store in an airtight container in the refrigerator for up to 2 weeks.

MAKES ABOUT 3 CUPS/700 ML.

LOW CARB

NUTRITIONAL ANALYSIS: Calories: **12**   Total fat: **>1g**   Saturated fat: **>1g**
% calories from fat: **4**   Carbohydrates: **3 g**   Protein: **>1 g**   Cholesterol: **0 mg**   Sodium: **>1 mg**

Butter & Herb Sauce

Sweet herbs in this sauce accent poultry or fish.

1/2 c./115 g.	**lowfat butter**
1/2 t./2.5 g.	**lemon zest**
2 T./30 ml.	**fresh lemon juice**
1 T./14 g.	**fresh parsley, finely minced**
1 t./5 g.	**fresh basil, minced**
1 t./5 g.	**fresh thyme, minced**
1 t./5 g.	**fresh sage, minced**

Whisk all ingredients in a small bowl. Brush on chicken or turkey before grilling.

MAKES 1/2 CUP/120 ML.

Steak Dipping Sauce

This full-bodied sauce provides plenty of flavor for any cut of beef.

8 oz./235 ml.	can tomato sauce
2 T./30 ml.	prepared yellow mustard
2 T./28 g.	dark brown sugar
2 T./30 ml.	low sodium soy sauce
2 T./30 ml.	cider vinegar
2 T./30 ml.	Worcestershire sauce
1 T./15 ml.	lemon juice
2	cloves garlic, finely minced
1	small white onion, finely chopped
1 T./14 g.	fresh parsley, finely minced

Combine all ingredients in a small saucepan and simmer over low heat for about 15 minutes. Sauce should be thickened slightly when done. Cool. Use immediately or store in an airtight container in the refrigerator for up to 2 weeks.

MAKES ABOUT 1 1/2 CUPS/360 ML.

LOW CARB

NUTRITIONAL ANALYSIS: Calories: **8**   Total fat: **>1g**   Saturated fat: **0g**
% calories from fat: **6**   Carbohydrates: **2 g**   Protein: **>1 g**   Cholesterol: **0 mg**   Sodium: **112 mg**

Sweet Cranberry Sauce

The perfect sauce to accompany grilled turkey breast.

1/2 c./115 g.	yellow/strong onion, finely chopped
2 T./30 ml.	cider vinegar
1/4 c./55 g.	dark molasses
8 oz./235 ml.	cranberry juice
8 oz./235 ml.	tomato sauce

Combine all ingredients in a small saucepan and simmer for 10 minutes. Do not allow the sauce to boil. Serve warm with poultry.

MAKES ABOUT 2 1/2 CUPS/600 ML.

NUTRITIONAL ANALYSIS: Calories: **12**   Total fat: **>1g**   Saturated fat: **0 g**
% calories from fat: **1**   Carbohydrates: **3 g**   Protein: **>1 g**   Cholesterol: **0 mg**   Sodium: **4 mg**

Quick & Easy Oriental Sauce

A super-fast spicy sauce. Use as a light dip for chicken or beef satay or to accompany pork chops.

1/2 c./120 ml.	**hoisin sauce**
1/2 c./120 ml.	**low sodium soy sauce**
1 t./5 ml.	**Asian chile oil**

Mix all the ingredients in a small saucepan and heat until warm, but not boiling. Simmer for 3 minutes to combine flavors. Serve warm.

MAKES ABOUT 1 CUP/250 ML.

NUTRITIONAL ANALYSIS: Calories: **18** Total fat: **>1g** Saturated fat: **0g** % calories from fat: **16** Carbohydrates: **3 g** Protein: **>1 g** Cholesterol: **0 mg** Sodium: **510 mg**

Honey Mustard Dipping Sauce

Pass this sauce with grilled chicken tenders.

1/2 c./120 ml.	**prepared yellow mustard**
2 T./30 ml.	**cider vinegar**
2	**cloves garlic, finely minced**
1/4 c./55 g.	**honey**
1 t./5 ml.	**lemon juice**
1/2 t./2.5 g.	**cayenne pepper**
1 T./14 g.	**lowfat butter**

Combine all the ingredients in a small saucepan. Heat for 4 minutes, or until the honey is completely dissolved and the sauce is slightly thickened. Serve warm.

MAKES ABOUT 3/4 CUP/210 ML.

NUTRITIONAL ANALYSIS: Calories: **24**   Total fat: **>1g**   Saturated fat: **>1g**
% calories from fat: **29**   Carbohydrates: **4 g**   Protein: **>1 g**   Cholesterol: **0 mg**   Sodium: **88 mg**

Sweet & Sour Sauce

Brush this sauce over grilled chicken, pork or vegetables for excellent flavor.

1 T./14 g.	cornstarch/cornflour
1 T./15 ml.	water
1 T./15 ml.	low sodium soy sauce
1/2 c./120 ml.	nonfat chicken broth/stock
1/4 c./60 ml.	cider vinegar
2 T./28 g.	clover honey
2 T./30 ml.	lemon juice
2 T./30 ml.	tomato paste

Combine the cornstarch and water in a small bowl. Set aside. In a small saucepan, combine the remaining ingredients. Heat and stir until bubbling. Slowly add the cornstarch-water mixture to the sauce. Simmer and stir for 3 minutes. The sauce will be thickened and smooth when done. Serve warm.

MAKES ABOUT 1 1/4 CUPS/300 ML.

LOW CARB

NUTRITIONAL ANALYSIS: Calories: **10**   Total fats: **0g**   Saturated fat: **0g**   % calories from fat: **0**   Carbohydrates: **2 g**   Protein: **>1 g**   Cholesterol: **0 mg**   Sodium: **49 mg**

Mango Tomato Salsa

Tart and sweet!

2 c./450 g.	**mangos, chopped**
3	**ripe tomatoes, chopped**
1/2 c./115 g.	**purple/red onion, finely chopped**
2 T./28 g.	**fresh cilantro/coriander leaves, finely minced**
2	**cloves garlic, finely minced**
1 T./15 ml.	**extra virgin olive oil**
1 T./15 ml.	**lemon juice**
1 T./15 ml.	**lime juice**
1/2 t./2.5 g.	**black pepper**
1/2 t./2.5 g.	**salt**

Lightly mix all ingredients in a medium-sized serving bowl. Chill to serve.

MAKES ABOUT 3 CUPS/700 ML.

NUTRITIONAL ANALYSIS: Calories: **8**   Total fat: **>1g**   Saturated fat: **0g**
% calories from fat: **28**   Carbohydrates: **1 g**   Protein: **>1 g**   Cholesterol: **0 mg**   Sodium: **20 mg**

Peach & Papaya Salsa

A colorful citrus complement for poultry or fish.

2 c./450 g.	peaches, chopped
2 c./450 g.	papayas, chopped
2 T./28 g.	honey
2 T./30 ml.	lemon juice
2 T./28 g.	purple/red onion, finely chopped
2 T./28 g.	fresh cilantro/coriander leaves, finely minced
1/2 t./2.5 g.	black pepper
1/2 t./2.5 g.	salt

Combine all the ingredients in a medium-sized serving bowl. Chill to serve.

MAKES 4 CUPS/1 LITRE SALSA.

NUTRITIONAL ANALYSIS: Calories: **7**   Total fat: **0g**   Saturated fat: **>1g**   % calories from fat: **2**   Carbohydrates: **2 g**   Protein: **>1 g**   Cholesterol: **0 mg**   Sodium: **20 mg**

RUBS
Heavy Duty Garlic Rub

Best with beef.

10	cloves garlic, finely minced
1 t./5 ml.	ketchup
1 t./5 g.	cracked black pepper
1/2 t./2.5 g.	salt
1 T./15 ml.	extra virgin olive oil

Mix all ingredients to make a thick paste. Generously press into all sides of the beef. Use immediately.

MAKES ENOUGH FOR 1 LARGE OR 2 SMALL STEAKS.

NUTRITIONAL ANALYSIS: Calories: **46** Total fat: **4g** Saturated fat: **>1g**
% calories from fat: **67** Carbohydrates: **3 g** Protein: **>1 g** Cholesterol: **0 mg** Sodium: **320 mg**

LOW CARB

Spicy Chicago Rub

For pork, beef or chicken.

1 T./14 g.	**black pepper**
1/4 c./55 g.	**ground paprika**
1 T./14 g.	**salt**
2 T./28 g.	**chili powder**
1 T./14 g.	**onion powder**
1 T./14 g.	**garlic powder**
1 T./14 g.	**dried parsley**
1/3 c./75 g.	**brown sugar**

Combine all ingredients in a small bowl. Mix thoroughly with a fork to evenly distribute the sugar. Store in an airtight container in the refrigerator for up to 3 months.

MAKES ABOUT 3/4 CUP/225 G.

NUTRITIONAL ANALYSIS: Calories: **42**   Total fat: **>1g**   Saturated fat: **>1g**   % calories from fat: **11**   Carbohydrates: **10 g**   Protein: **>1 g**   Cholesterol: **0 mg**   Sodium: **642 mg**

Southern Onion Rub

Dehydrated onions give this rub an exciting flavor!

2 T./28 g.	**dehydrated minced onions**
1/4 c./55 g.	**ground paprika**
1 T./14 g.	**black pepper**
2 t./10 g.	**cayenne pepper**
2 t./10 g.	**onion powder**
1 t./5 g.	**salt**

Combine all ingredients in a small bowl. Store in an airtight container in the refrigerator for up to 3 months.

MAKES ABOUT 1/2 CUP/120 G.

NUTRITIONAL ANALYSIS: Calories: **27**   Total fat: **1g**   Saturated fat: **>1g**   % calories from fat: **25**   Carbohydrates: **7 g**   Protein: **2 g**   Cholesterol: **0 mg**   Sodium: **321 mg**

Chicken Paprika Rub

This rub gives grilled chicken a beautiful color and spicy taste.

1/2 c./115 g.	**ground paprika**
1 T./14 g.	**dried parsley**
2 T./28 g.	**onion powder**
1 T./14 g.	**cayenne pepper**
2 t./10 g.	**black pepper, coarsely ground**
1 t./5 g.	**salt**

Combine all ingredients in a small bowl. Store in an airtight container in the refrigerator for up to 3 months.

MAKES ABOUT 3/4 CUP/185 G.

NUTRITIONAL ANALYSIS: Calories: **33**   Total fat: **1g**   Saturated **fat: >1g**
% calories from fat: **25**   Carbohydrates: **7 g**   Protein: **2 g**   Cholesterol: **0 mg**   Sodium: **320 mg**

Southwest Rub

Flavors that capture the West and Mexico.

1/2 t./2.5 g.	**ground cumin**
1/2 t./2.5 g.	**ground cinnamon**
1/2 t./2.5 g.	**ground coriander**
1 t./5 g.	**ground paprika**
1 t./5 g.	**chili powder**
1/2 t./2.5 g.	**cayenne pepper**
1 T./14 g.	**black pepper**
1 T./14 g.	**garlic salt**

Combine all ingredients in a small bowl. Store in an airtight container in the refrigerator for up to 3 months.

MAKES ABOUT 1/2 CUP/100 G.

NUTRITIONAL ANALYSIS: Calories: **24**   Total fat: **>1g**   Saturated fat:° **>1g**
% calories from fat: **21** Carbohydrates: **5 g** Protein: **1 g** Cholesterol: **0 mg** Sodium: **236 mg**

Three Alarm Rub

A hot, hot, hot rub that is great with beef and lamb.

1 T./14 g.	**cayenne pepper**
2 T./28 g.	**black pepper**
2 T./28 g.	**chili powder**
2 T./28 g.	**onion powder**
2 T./28 g.	**garlic powder**
1 T./14 g.	**salt**
1 T./14 g.	**sugar**
1/4 c./55 g.	**ground paprika**

Combine all ingredients in a small bowl. Store in an airtight container in the refrigerator for up to 3 months.

MAKES ABOUT 1 CUP/200 G.

NUTRITIONAL ANALYSIS: Calories: **38**   Total fat: **>1g**   Saturated fat: **>1g**
% calories from fat: **17**   Carbohydrates: **8 g**   Protein: **1 g**   Cholesterol: **0 mg**   Sodium: **827 mg**

Italian Pork Rub

Perfect for pork chops!

1/2 t./2.5 g.	black pepper
1/2 t./2.5 g.	cayenne pepper
1/4 c./55 g.	ground paprika
2 t./10 g.	dried oregano
2 t./10 g.	garlic powder
2 t./10 g.	onion powder
2 t./10 g.	dried Italian seasoning
1 t./5 g.	salt

Combine all ingredients in a small bowl. Store in an airtight container in the refrigerator for up to 3 months.

MAKES ABOUT 1/4 CUP/100 G.

NUTRITIONAL ANALYSIS: Calories: **34**   Total fat: **>1g**   Saturated fat: **>1g**
% calories from fat: **21**   Carbohydrates: **7 g**   Protein: **1 g**   Cholesterol: **0 mg**   Sodium: **572 mg**

Mustard Pepper Rub

Great with pork or beef.

1 T./14 g.	dry mustard
1/4 c./55 g.	ground paprika
2 T./28 g.	black pepper
1 T./14 g.	cayenne pepper
1 T./14 g.	sugar

Combine all ingredients in a small bowl. Store in an airtight container in the refrigerator for up to 3 months.

MAKES ABOUT 1/2 CUP/125 G.

LOW CARB

NUTRITIONAL ANALYSIS: Calories: **47** Total fat: **2g** Saturated fat: **>1g**
% calories from fat: **27** Carbohydrates: **9 g** Protein: **2 g** Cholesterol: **0 mg** Sodium: **4 mg**

Savory Spice Rub

A lovely blend of spices to accompany grilled vegetables.

1 T./14 g.	black pepper
2 t./10 g.	cayenne pepper
1 t./5 g.	dried oregano
1 t./5 g.	dried basil
1 T./14 g.	ground paprika
2 T./28 g.	light brown sugar
1 T./14 g.	salt
2 t./10 g.	garlic powder
2 t./10 g.	onion powder
1 T./14 g.	chili powder

Combine all ingredients in a small bowl. Store in an airtight container in the refrigerator for up to 3 months.

MAKES ABOUT 1/2 CUP/120 G.

NUTRITIONAL ANALYSIS: Calories: **35**   Total fat: **>1g**   Saturated fat: **>1g**
% calories from fat: **14**   Carbohydrates: **8 g**   Protein: **>1 g**   Cholesterol: **0 mg**   Sodium: **1,348 mg**

Lemon Pepper Rub

Partners beautifully with fish and poultry.

2 t./10 g.	lemon pepper
1 t./5 ml.	lemon juice
2 t./10 g.	fresh rosemary, minced
1 T./14 g.	fresh dill, finely minced
1 t./5 g.	salt
1 t./5 g.	black pepper
2	cloves garlic, finely minced

Combine all ingredients in a small bowl. Use immediately as a rub for fish or poultry. Discard leftovers.

MAKES ABOUT 1/4 CUP/55 G.

NUTRITIONAL ANALYSIS: Calories: **15**   Total fat: **>1g**   Saturated fat: **>1g**   % calories from fat: **14**   Carbohydrates: **3 g**   Protein: **>1 g**   Cholesterol: **0 mg**   Sodium: **1,752 mg**

CHAPTER

A CUT ABOVE
—Beef & Lamb

Beef is one of the world's most highly prized meats and is a great choice for the grill. Your *George Foreman® Lean Mean Fat Reducing Grilling Machine* makes it very easy to grill a perfect steak or burger. But, you can't live on that alone, so we've created recipes in this chapter using many cuts of beef that offer the rich flavor you want with less fat than you would imagine. Tenderloin, flank/skirt steak, London broil, top and bottom round steak and lean hamburger are some cuts that make sense when you're looking for great beef choices.

We've also included recipes using lamb in this chapter. Lamb is full of flavor and grills well in *The George Foreman® Lean Mean Fat Reducing Grilling Machine*. Inside these pages you'll find classic lamb recipes using garlic and rosemary and you'll discover a few surprises in lamb recipes paired with vegetables or fruit.

To ensure that your grilled beef and lamb does not overcook, check the meat a few minutes before it should be done. It's easy to continue grilling meat that is too rare, but impossible to correct overcooked meat. If the meat is not the same thickness throughout the entire cut, you may find that part of the meat shows grill "char marks" and another part may not. You may turn the meat around to "even" these marks, if you like, but the marks will not affect the flavor or result of the grilled meat.

Use a heat-tolerant plastic fork or the plastic grilling spatula whenever you choose to reposition meat. You may find that if you have several uneven pieces of meat in the grill, some pieces may grill more quickly than others. If this occurs, reposition the meat in the grill, or remove some portions and allow others to grill for an extra minute or so.

If you are grilling for more than one person, it is likely that each person will prefer a different degree of "doneness." Set the Timer for the rarest choice and continue grilling as needed. Don't worry about turning over any cut of meat because the grill cooks both sides of the meat at the same time.

To make kebabs, use wooden skewers only and we recommend that you soak them first in water for about 20 minutes. Drain them and use them as directed in each recipe. Soaking the skewers in water first allows food to slide more easily on and off the skewers and also keeps the skewers from burning in the grill as the food cooks.

BEEF STEAKS & CUTS
Mushroom Tenderloin Steaks

A tasty entrée for a busy weeknight.

4	**4 oz.**/115 g. **beef tenderloin/filet steaks**
1 T./14 g.	**parsley, finely minced**
1	**clove garlic, finely minced**
1 t./5 g.	**salt**
1/2 t./2.5 g.	**black pepper**
4 oz./115 g.	**fresh or canned mushroom slices, drained**

Set the Temperature to 400ºF/200ºC and allow the grill to preheat. Remove any visible fat from the steaks. Sprinkle each steak with the parsley, garlic, salt and pepper. Place the steaks in the grill and set the Timer to 4 minutes for medium-rare steaks. Spoon the mushroom slices over the steaks and grill for an additional 1–2 minutes.

SERVES 4.

NUTRITIONAL ANALYSIS: Calories: **145** Total fat: **5g** Saturated fat: **2g**
% calories from fat: **33** Carbohydrates: **2 g** Protein: **22 g** Cholesterol: **62 mg** Sodium: **750 mg**

Southwestern Rubbed Steak

Use spices generously to make this steak special!

1 lb./450 g.	**beef tenderloin steak**
1 t./5 g.	**salt**
1 T./14 g.	**brown sugar**
1/2 t./2.5 g.	**ground cumin**
1 t./5 g.	**chili powder**
1/2 t./2.5 g.	**cayenne pepper**

Remove any visible fat from the steak. Mix together the salt, sugar, cumin, chili powder and cayenne pepper. Press the spices firmly onto all sides of the steak and let stand for 5 minutes.

Set the Temperature to 400°F/200°C and allow the grill to preheat. Place the steak in the grill and set the Timer to 5 minutes for medium, or to 6 minutes for well-done steak. Cut the steak into 4 portions or slice thinly and serve on a warm platter.

SERVES 4.

NUTRITIONAL ANALYSIS: Calories: **148**   Total fat: **5g**   Saturated fat: **2g**
% calories from fat: **33**   Carbohydrates: **3 g**   Protein: **21 g**   Cholesterol: **62 mg**   Sodium: **635 mg**

Spicy Pepper Steak

Accompany this steak with creamy risotto and a fresh green salad and dinner is done!

1 lb./450 g.	**beef bottom round steak**
1 t./5 g.	**salt**
1/2 t./2.5 g.	**pepper**
1/4 t./1 g.	**cayenne pepper**
1	**green pepper, seeded and sliced into thin rings**
1	**red pepper, seeded and sliced into thin rings**
1	**white onion, sliced into thin rings**

Set the Temperature to 400ºF/200ºC and allow the grill to preheat. Remove any visible fat from the steak and cut diagonally across the grain into thin slices. Place the steak slices in the grill and sprinkle with the salt, pepper and cayenne pepper. Set the Timer to 2 minutes and grill the steak to very rare. When the Timer beeps, add the peppers and the onion slices. Set the Timer to 2 minutes and grill until the vegetables are tender-crisp.

SERVES 4.

NUTRITIONAL ANALYSIS: Calories: **183**   Total fat: **7g**   Saturated fat: **3g**
% calories from fat: **34**   Carbohydrates: **7 g**   Protein: **23 g**   Cholesterol: **66 mg**   Sodium: **619 mg**

Grilled Asian Beef

Marinate these steaks for full flavor.

4	**6 oz.**/170 g. **beef ribeye/T-bone (short end) steaks**
1/2 c./120 ml.	**low sodium soy sauce**
2	**cloves garlic, finely minced**
1 T./15 ml.	**vegetable oil**
1 T./15 ml.	**white vinegar**
1 T./14 g.	**brown sugar**
1 t./5 g.	**ground ginger**

Remove any visible fat from the steaks and place the steaks in a flat glass pan. Combine the soy sauce, garlic, oil, vinegar, sugar and ginger in a small bowl and mix well. Pour over the steaks and marinate for at least 1 hour.

Set the Temperature to 400°F/200°C and allow the grill to preheat. Set the Timer to 5 minutes and grill the steaks to medium-rare. When the Timer beeps, check the steaks and continue grilling if desired.

SERVES 4.

LOW CARB

NUTRITIONAL ANALYSIS: Calories: **207**   Total fat: **9g**   Saturated fat: **4g**   % calories from fat: **43**   Carbohydrates: **6 g**   Protein: **20 g**   Cholesterol: **52 mg**   Sodium: **1,113 mg**

Onion Butter London Broil

For best results, grill until the beef is rare or medium-rare.

1 1/2 lb./680 g.	**London broil beef/skirt steak, 1 1/2-inch**/3.75 cm. **thick**
1/2 c./115 g.	**lowfat margarine**
1 t./5 ml.	**Worcestershire sauce**
1	**clove garlic, finely minced**
2 T./28 g.	**fresh parsley, finely minced**
2 T./28 g.	**green/spring onions, finely chopped**

Set the Temperature to 400ºF/200ºC and allow the grill to preheat. In a small bowl, combine the margarine and Worcestershire sauce. Blend well. Add the garlic, parsley and green onions. Remove any visible fat from the steak and place the steak in the grill.

Close the grill and set the Timer for 3 minutes. When the Timer beeps, open the grill and brush the butter-herb sauce over the steak. Set the Timer for 3 minutes and continue grilling. As the butter sauce melts, it will run into the drip tray. To serve, slice thinly across the grain and arrange on a warm platter. Pour the melted butter sauce from the drip tray over the sliced beef.

SERVES 6.

NUTRITIONAL ANALYSIS: Calories: **217**   Total fat: **13g**   Saturated fat: **5g**
% calories from fat: **59**   Carbohydrates: **1 g**   Protein: **18 g**   Cholesterol: **52 mg**   Sodium: **156 mg**

Sunday Beef Kebabs

Tender beef combines with fresh vegetables and a touch of Oriental sauce.

1 lb./450 g.	**beef sirloin, cut into 1-inch**/2.5 cm **cubes**
1 c./225 g.	**fresh or canned pineapple chunks**
8	**cherry tomatoes**
1	**green pepper, cut into 1-inch**/2.5 cm **pieces**
8	**button mushrooms, cleaned**
1/4 c./60 ml.	**low sodium soy sauce**
2 T./28 g.	**honey**
1/2 t./2.5 g.	**ground ginger**
1 T./14 g.	**garlic, finely minced**
8	**10-inch**/25 cm **wooden skewers, soaked in water and drained**

Thread the meat onto 4 skewers. Thread the pineapple, tomatoes, green pepper and mushrooms onto 4 skewers, alternating each. In a small bowl, mix the soy sauce, honey, ginger and garlic. Brush the sauce over the beef and the vegetables.

Set the Temperature to 350ºF/170ºC and allow the grill to preheat. Place the beef skewers in the grill widthwise (horizontally) and set the Timer for 3 minutes. When the Timer beeps, open the grill and add the vegetable skewers widthwise. Close the grill and set the Timer for an additional 3 minutes.

SERVES 4.

NUTRITIONAL   ANALYSIS: Calories: **226**   Total fat: **5g**   Saturated fat: **2g**
% calories from fat: **19**   Carbohydrates: **20 g**   Protein: **26 g**   Cholesterol: **68 mg**   Sodium: **610 mg**

Milano Sirloin Steaks

A little bit of Italy!

1 lb./450 g.	**beef sirloin steaks**
2 T./28 g.	**fresh basil, finely minced**
1/2 t./2.5 g.	**dried oregano**
1 t./5 g.	**black pepper**
1/2 t./2.5 g.	**salt**
2 c./450 g.	**red tomatoes, coarsely chopped**

Set the Temperature to 400ºF/200ºC and allow the grill to preheat. Remove any visible fat from the steaks. Place the steaks in the grill and sprinkle with the basil, oregano, pepper and salt.

Set the Timer to 4 minutes and close the grill. When the Timer beeps, add the tomatoes and grill for 1 minute. As the tomatoes grill, the juice will collect in the drip tray. If desired, you may pour the juice over the grilled steaks to serve.

SERVES 4.

NUTRITIONAL ANALYSIS: Calories: **157**   Total fat: **5g**   Saturated fat: **2g**
% calories from fat: **31**   Carbohydrates: **5 g**   Protein: **22 g**   Cholesterol: **62 mg**   Sodium: **345 mg**

LOW CARB

Dijon Flank Steak

Grill with Vidalia/mild onions for a perfect dinner.

1 1/2 lb./680 g.	**beef flank/skirt steak**
1 T./15 ml.	**Dijon mustard**
1/4 c./60 ml.	**cider vinegar**
1 t./5 g.	**salt**
1/2 t./2.5 g.	**black pepper**
1	**Vidalia/mild onion, thinly sliced**

Remove any visible fat from the steak and place the steak in a flat glass pan. In a small bowl, combine the mustard, vinegar, salt and pepper and pour over the steak. Refrigerate, covered, for 30 minutes.

Set the Temperature to 400ºF/200ºC and allow the grill to preheat. Place the steak in the grill and set the Timer to 4 minutes. Grill until the Timer beeps, add the sliced onion and set the Timer for 2 minutes. When the Timer beeps, remove the beef and onion and let stand for 5 minutes. Slice the beef thinly across the grain and serve topped with the onions.

SERVES 6.

NUTRITIONAL ANALYSIS: Calories: **180** Total fat: **8g** Saturated fat: **4g** % calories from fat: **43** Carbohydrates: **3 g** Protein: **22 g** Cholesterol: **54 mg** Sodium: **519 mg**

Hawaiian Pineapple Beef
Flavorful and delicious!

1 1/2 lb./680 g.	**London broil beef/hindquarter flank steak**
2 T./28 g.	**green/spring onion, finely minced**
1 t./5 g.	**ground ginger**
1 T./14 g.	**honey**
1/2 c./115 g.	**fresh pineapple, cut into small pieces**
	(substitute canned pineapple chunks, drained)

Remove any visible fat from the steak. In a small bowl, combine the green/spring onion, ginger, honey and mix well. Set the Temperature to 400ºF/200ºC and allow the grill to preheat. Place the steak in the grill and spoon the sauce over the steak. Set the Timer for 3 minutes.

Grill until the Timer beeps, add the pineapple pieces on top of and around the steak and grill for 3 minutes. To serve, slice the steak thinly across the grain and spoon the warm pineapple over the top.

SERVES 6.

NUTRITIONAL ANALYSIS: Calories: **193**   Total fat: **6g**   Saturated fat: **4g**   % calories from fat: **33**   Carbohydrates: **5 g**   Protein: **23 g**   Cholesterol: **65 mg**   Sodium: **70 mg**

Stuffed Steak Olé

A delectable combination of grilled beef and fresh vegetable salsa.

2 lbs./900 g.	beef flank/skirt steak
2 c./450 g.	fresh tomato, chopped
1/4 c./55 g.	fresh cilantro/coriander leaves, finely minced
2	cloves garlic, finely minced
1/2 c./115 g.	yellow/strong onion, chopped
1/4 c./55 g.	green pepper, chopped
1/2 t./2.5 g.	ground cumin
1/2 t./2.5 g.	cayenne pepper
1/2 t./2.5 g.	salt

Remove any visible fat from the steak. With a sharp knife, cut a slit sideways into the steak to create a pocket, without cutting completely through the meat. In a medium bowl, combine the tomato, cilantro/coriander leaves, garlic, onion, green pepper, cumin, pepper and salt. Mix well and stuff the pocket of the steak with the vegetable-herb salsa. Press the sides of the steak to close or secure with toothpicks, if desired.

Set the Temperature to 400ºF/200ºC and allow the grill to preheat. Place the steak in the grill and set the Timer to 7 minutes. When the Timer beeps, check the steak and continue grilling if desired. To serve, cut the steak across the grain into 1/4-inch/6 mm. slices. Top the slices with any remaining vegetable-herb salsa.

SERVES 6.

NUTRITIONAL ANALYSIS: Calories: **262** Total fat: **12g** Saturated fat: **5g** % calories from fat: **42** Carbohydrates: **5 g** Protein: **32 g** Cholesterol: **78 mg** Sodium: **298 mg**

T-bone Steaks with Barbeque Butter

T-bone steaks are juicy and delicious, but they can also be very high in fat. To control that fat, use a sharp knife to remove as much visible fat as possible and keep portions small.

4	**6 oz.**/170 g. **beef T-bone steaks**
2 T./30 ml.	**Worcestershire sauce**
1/4 c./55 g.	**lowfat margarine**
1/4 c./55 g.	**green/spring onions, chopped**
1 t./5 g.	**salt**
1/4 t./1 g.	**black pepper**

Remove any visible fat from the steaks. Set the Temperature to 400°F/200°C and allow the grill to preheat. In a small bowl, combine the Worcestershire sauce, margarine, green onions, salt and pepper. Place the steaks in the grill and cover each with the barbeque butter.

Set the Timer to 5 minutes and grill to medium-rare, or grill for an additional 1-2 minutes, if desired. As the butter melts, it will run into the drip tray.

SERVES 4.

NUTRITIONAL ANALYSIS: Calories: **208**   Total fat: **10g**   Saturated fat: **4g**
% calories from fat: **47**   Carbohydrates: **3 g**   Protein: **23 g**   Cholesterol: **65 mg**   Sodium: **796 mg**

LOW CARB

Teriyaki Beef

Serve over steamed rice for a traditional delight.

1 lb./450 g.	lean beef (such as flank/skirt steak, or bottom round/top side)
1/4 c./60 ml.	sesame oil
1/4 c./60 ml.	low sodium soy sauce
1/4 c./60 ml.	cider vinegar
2 T./28 g.	honey
2 T./28 g.	green/spring onion, chopped
2	cloves garlic, chopped
1 t./5 g.	ground ginger

Remove any visible fat from the beef and place the steak in a flat glass pan. Combine the oil, soy sauce, vinegar, honey, onion, garlic and ginger and pour over the meat. Cover tightly and marinate in the refrigerator for 2–12 hours.

Set the Temperature to 400ºF/200ºC and allow the grill to preheat. Place the steak in the grill. Set the Timer to 6 minutes and grill the steak to medium, or grill for an additional 1-2 minutes, according to your preference. Slice thinly across the grain of the beef. If you choose to use the marinade as a sauce, boil it for 5 minutes before serving.

SERVES 4.

NUTRITIONAL ANALYSIS: Calories: **359**   Total fat: **23g**   Saturated fat: **6g**
% calories from fat: **56** Carbohydrates: **14 g** Protein: **26 g** Cholesterol: **59 mg** Sodium: **1,065 mg**

Mediterranean Beef & Vegetable Grill

Tempting and colorful for a summer evening meal.

1 lb./450 g.	**beef flank/skirt steak**
1	**small zucchini/courgette, cut into 1-inch**/2.5 cm **cubes**
1	**small tomato, cut into 8 pieces**
1/4	**white onion, cut into 1⁄4-inch**/6 mm **pieces**
1	**green pepper, cut into 1⁄4-inch**/ 6 mm **pieces**
1 T./15 ml.	**balsamic vinegar**
1 t./5 g.	**black pepper, coarsely ground**
1 t./5 g.	**garlic salt**
8	**10-inch**/25 cm **wooden skewers, soaked in water and drained**

Partially freeze the flank/skirt steak (for about 30 minutes). Remove any visible fat and cut the beef into very thin slices across the grain of the meat. Thread the steak through 4 of the skewers in an accordion fashion. Set aside. Thread the vegetables through the remaining 4 skewers, alternating vegetables on each. In a small bowl, mix together the vinegar, pepper and garlic salt.

Set the Temperature to 400ºF/200ºC and allow the grill to preheat. Place the beef skewers in the grill widthwise (horizontally) and set the Timer for 3 minutes. Grill until the Timer beeps, add the vegetable skewers (widthwise) and sprinkle each meat and vegetable skewer with the vinegar, pepper and garlic salt mixture. Grill for an additional 3–4 minutes. **SERVES 4.**

NUTRITIONAL ANALYSIS: Calories: **203**   Total fat: **9g**   Saturated fat: **4g**
% calories from fat: **40**   Carbohydrates: **5 g**   Protein: **25 g**   Cholesterol: **59 mg**   Sodium: **530 mg**

Pepper Crusted Steak

The rich flavor of steak mingles with a spicy pepper crust.

1 lb./450 g.	**beef flank/skirt steak**
2 T./28 g.	**black pepper, coarsely ground**
1 t./5 g.	**seasoned salt**
1 t./5 g.	**garlic powder**
1 T./14 g.	**fresh parsley, finely minced**

Remove any visible fat from the steak. Combine the pepper, salt, garlic powder and parsley and press firmly into all sides of the steak.

Set the Temperature to 400ºF/200ºC and allow the grill to preheat. Place the steak in the grill and set the Timer to 6 minutes for medium steak, or continue grilling according to your preference. To serve, slice thinly across the grain.

SERVES 4.

LOW CARB

NUTRITIONAL ANALYSIS: Calories: **192**   Total fat: **9g**   Saturated fat: **4g**
% calories from fat: **43**   Carbohydrates: **3 g**   Protein: **24 g**   Cholesterol: **59 mg**   Sodium: **422 mg**

Lime Steak Fajitas

In the true style of Mexico, a bit of tender meat is added to fresh vegetables and toppings to create a memorable meal.

1/2 lb./225 g.	**beef flank/skirt steak**
1/3 c./80 ml.	**lime juice**
1 t./5 g.	**black pepper**
1/2 t./2.5 g.	**cayenne pepper**
1	**green pepper**
1	**red pepper**
1	**small white onion**
8	**flour tortillas, warmed**
1/2 c./115 g.	**lowfat cheddar cheese, shredded**
1/2 c./120 ml.	**lowfat sour cream**

Remove any visible fat from the steak. Cut the steak into very thin slices and place in a flat glass pan. Mix together the lime juice and black pepper and pour over the steak. Refrigerate for 2–4 hours. Remove the seeds and inner fibers from the green and red peppers and cut into very thin slices. Cut the onion into thin slices and separate the rings.

Set the Temperature to 400ºF/200ºC and allow the grill to preheat. Place the steak in the grill and set the Timer for 3 minutes. When the Timer beeps, place the peppers and onion over the top of the steak and grill for 3–4 minutes. To serve, fill the tortillas with the meat and vegetables and pass the cheese and sour cream to add as desired.

SERVES 8.

NUTRITIONAL ANALYSIS: Calories: **254** Total fat: **8g** Saturated fat: **3g** % calories from fat: **27** Carbohydrates: **32 g** Protein: **14 g** Cholesterol: **21 mg** Sodium: **314 mg**

BEEF RIBS
Oriental Beef Short Ribs

Tender and juicy!

3 lbs./1.4 kg	beef short ribs
1	clove garlic, finely chopped
1/2 c./120 ml.	low sodium soy sauce
1 t./5 ml.	sesame oil
1 t./5 g.	ground ginger
2 T./28 g.	honey
1 T./15 ml.	cider vinegar

Parboil/steam the ribs for 20 minutes. (To parboil ribs: cook the ribs for 20 minutes in a steamer rack over a pan of boiling water). Cool and remove any visible fat. Place the ribs in a flat glass pan. In a small bowl, blend the garlic, soy sauce, oil, ginger, honey and vinegar until the honey is dissolved. Pour the marinade over the ribs, cover the pan tightly and refrigerate for 2–12 hours.

Set the Temperature to 350ºF/170ºC and allow the grill to preheat. Place the ribs in the grill and set the Timer to 7 minutes. When the Timer beeps, check the ribs and continue grilling if desired. When done, the ribs should be lightly charred and the meat completely cooked.

SERVES 4.

NUTRITIONAL ANALYSIS: Calories: **295**   Total fat: **14g**   Saturated fat: **7g**   % calories from fat: **44**   Carbohydrates: **12 g**   Protein: **29 g**   Cholesterol: **82 mg**   Sodium: **1,118 mg**

Classic BBQ Beef Ribs

A rich sauce coats these juicy ribs.

5 lbs./2.25 kg	**beef loin ribs (12–15 ribs)**
1/2 c./120 ml.	**ketchup**
2 T./30 ml.	**prepared mustard**
1 T./15 ml.	**Worcestershire sauce**
1	**clove garlic, finely minced**
1 T./14 g.	**brown sugar**

Parboil/steam the ribs for 20 minutes. (To parboil ribs: cook the ribs for 20 minutes in a steamer rack over a pan of boiling water). Cool and remove any visible fat from the ribs. In a small bowl, combine the ketchup, mustard, Worcestershire sauce, garlic and brown sugar.

Set the Temperature to 350ºF/170ºC and allow the grill to preheat. Place the ribs in the grill and set the Timer to 2 minutes. When the Timer beeps, baste the ribs with the sauce. Close the grill and set the Timer for 2 minutes. When the Timer beeps, baste again, turning the ribs to coat thoroughly. Close the grill and set the Timer for 2 minutes. To serve, pass the remaining sauce with the ribs.

SERVES 6.

NUTRITIONAL ANALYSIS: Calories: **518** Total fat: **29g** Saturated fat: **15g** % calories from fat: **51** Carbohydrates: **8 g** Protein: **55 g** Cholesterol: **181 mg** Sodium: **475 mg**

LAMB CHOPS
Dijon Citrus Lamb Chops

Orange and mustard flavors accent these tender chops.

4	**4–6 oz.**/120-170 g. **lamb loin chops**
1/4 c./60 ml.	**Dijon mustard**
1 T./15 ml.	**orange juice**
1 t./5 g.	**brown sugar**
1/2 t./2.5 g.	**black pepper**
1/4 t./1 g.	**salt**
2	**sweet oranges, peeled and cut into 1/2-inch**/13 mm **rings**

Remove any visible fat from the lamb chops. In a small bowl, blend the mustard, juice, sugar, pepper and salt. Set the Temperature to 350ºF/170ºC and allow the grill to preheat. Place the chops in the grill and cover each with the mustard-orange sauce.

Set the Timer to 4 minutes and grill to medium-rare, or continue grilling according to your preference. Arrange the orange slices on 4 plates and place a lamb chop on top of each.

SERVES 4.

Garlic Lamb & New Potatoes

This recipe originated in Greece, where lamb is highly prized for its tenderness and flavor.

4	**4–6 oz.**/120-170 g. **lamb loin chops**
2	**cloves garlic, finely minced**
2 T./30 ml.	**lemon juice**
1 T./15 ml.	**extra virgin olive oil**
1 T./14 g.	**fresh rosemary, finely minced**
1 t./5 g.	**black pepper, coarsely ground**
4	**small new potatoes**
4	**fresh mushrooms, thinly sliced**
1 t./5 ml.	**extra virgin olive oil**
1 t./5 g.	**salt**
1/2 t./2.5 g.	**black pepper**

Remove any visible fat from the chops and place the chops in a flat glass pan. Combine the garlic, lemon juice, 1 tablespoon/15 ml. oil, rosemary and 1 teaspoon/5 g. of black pepper in a small bowl and pour over the chops. Cover tightly and marinate in the refrigerator for 2–8 hours. Scrub the potatoes and slice into 1/4-inch/6 mm rounds.

Set the Temperature to 350ºF/170ºC and allow the grill to preheat. Place the potatoes and mushrooms in the grill and sprinkle with the remaining oil, salt and pepper. Set the Timer for 5 minutes. Grill until the Timer beeps, move the potatoes and mushrooms to the edges of the grill, and place the lamb chops in the center of the grill. Grill the lamb and vegetables for 4–6 minutes, or until the chops are rare to medium and the potatoes are tender. **SERVES 4.**

NUTRITIONAL ANALYSIS: Calories: **307** Total fat: **13g** Saturated fat: **4g**
% calories from fat: **37** Carbohydrates: **26 g** Protein: **23 g** Cholesterol: **67 mg** Sodium: **636 mg**

Raspberry & Mint Lamb Chops

A hint of sweetness complements the chops.

4	**4–6 oz.**/120-170 g. **lamb loin chops**
2 T./30 ml.	**raspberry jelly**
1 t./5 g.	**fresh mint, finely minced**
1 t./5 ml.	**extra virgin olive oil**
1	**clove garlic, finely minced**

Remove any visible fat from the chops. Set the Temperature to 350°F/170°C and allow the grill to preheat. In a small bowl, combine the jelly, mint, oil and garlic.

Place the chops in the grill and spoon the sauce over each. Set the Timer for 4 minutes for medium-rare lamb, or continue grilling according to your preference.

SERVES 4.

NUTRITIONAL ANALYSIS: Calories: **191**   Total fat: **9g**   Saturated fat: **3g**
% calories from fat: **43**   Carbohydrates: **7 g**   Protein: **20 g**   Cholesterol: **67 mg**   Sodium: **47 mg**

Grilled Lamb Chops with Papaya Peach Salsa

Count on this tangy salsa to awaken your appetite.

4	**4–6 oz.**/120-170 g.	**lamb loin chops**
1 t./5 g.		**black pepper, coarsely ground**
1/2 t./2.5 g.		**salt**
2 c./450 g.		**ripe papayas, chopped**
1 c./225 g.		**ripe peaches, chopped**
1 T./14 g.		**red onion, chopped**
2 T./28 g.		**fresh cilantro/coriander leaves, chopped**
1 T./15 ml.		**lemon juice**
1/4 t./1 g.		**salt**

Remove all visible fat from the chops. Set the Temperature to 350ºF/170ºC and allow the grill to preheat. Place the chops in the grill and sprinkle with the pepper and 1/2 teaspoon/2.5 g. of salt. Set the Timer to 4 minutes for medium-rare, or continue grilling according to your preference.

In a medium serving bowl, mix together thoroughly the papayas, peaches, onion, cilantro/coriander leaves, lemon juice and 1/4 teaspoon/1 g. salt. To serve, place one lamp chop on each plate and cover with the salsa.

SERVES 4.

NUTRITIONAL ANALYSIS: Calories: **204**   Total fat: **8g**   Saturated fat: **3g**
% calories from fat: **35**   Carbohydrates: **13 g**   Protein: **21 g**   Cholesterol: **67 mg**   Sodium: **481 mg**

Moroccan Lamb Kebabs

These beautiful kebabs make any meal a special occasion.

1 T./15 ml.	**extra virgin olive oil**
2 T./30 ml.	**lemon juice**
2 T./30 ml.	**water**
2 T./30 ml.	**balsamic vinegar**
1 t./5 g.	**black pepper, coarsely ground**
1	**clove garlic, finely minced**
1 t./5 g.	**fresh oregano, minced**
1 lb./450 g.	**boneless lamb**
1	**zucchini/courgette, cleaned**
12	**button mushrooms, scrubbed**
8	**cherry tomatoes**
8	**10-inch**/25 cm **wooden skewers**

In a small bowl combine the oil, lemon juice, water, vinegar, pepper, garlic and oregano. Place the lamb in a glass pan and pour the marinade over the meat. Cover and refrigerate for 2–6 hours.

Thread the lamb and vegetables on the skewers, alternating each. Set the Temperature to 350°F/170°C and allow the grill to preheat. Place the kebabs in the grill widthwise (horizontally) and set the Timer for 7 minutes. When the Timer beeps, check the lamb and continue grilling if desired.

SERVES 4.

LOW CARB

NUTRITIONAL ANALYSIS: Calories: **156** Total fat: **9g** Saturated fat: **2g**
% calories from fat: **49** Carbohydrates: **9 g** Protein: **12 g** Cholesterol: **33 mg** Sodium: **621 mg**

SMOKY SENSATIONS
—Pork Chops, Ribs & Ham

From pork ribs and chops to grilled ham slices, you'll love the satisfying flavor of pork grilled in *The George Foreman® Lean Mean Fat Reducing Grilling Machine*. Pork has an even texture and a mild taste that agrees with many ingredients. However, pork cuts differ widely in fat content, ranging from 7 fat grams in a tenderloin/filet to a whopping 56 fat grams for a standard serving of country-style pork ribs.

In this chapter you'll find recipes that will highlight chops, ribs, tenderloin/filet and ham, and we'll also offer some ways to reduce the fat in the pork as you prepare it. If you are following a high-protein, low-carb diet, look for the "LOW CARB" icon in special recipes.

Pork should be well done when prepared in the grill (about 160°F/71°C) to avoid possible contamination. However, pork becomes dry and tough if you overcook it, so watch pork carefully as it grills. Check it a few minutes before it's supposed to be done and time it accordingly.

Ribs are a favorite pork specialty and we prepare them in our recipes by parboiling them first. Parboiling separates the meat from the fat on each rib, which means less fat in your grilled meat.

Directions for parboiling are included in each recipe for ribs. Even though parboiling adds a bit of time to your preparation, we think you'll agree with us that the results are well worth it.

PORK TENDERLOIN & CHOPS
Grilled Pork with Peach Salsa

Marinated tenderloin/filet combines with a snappy salsa!

4	**6 oz./170 g. pork tenderloin/filets**
1 t./5 ml.	**vegetable oil**
1 T./14 g.	**honey**
2 T./30 ml.	**low sodium soy sauce**
1 T./15 ml.	**cider vinegar**
1 t./5 g.	**ground ginger**
1/4 t./1 g.	**ground cinnamon**
2 T./28 g.	**apricot marmalade**
3	**peaches, peeled and cut into 1/2-inch/ 12 mm pieces**
1/4 c./55 g.	**red onion, chopped**
2 T./28 g.	**fresh parsley, minced**

Remove any visible fat from the pork. Place the pork in a flat glass pan. Combine the oil, honey, soy sauce and vinegar and pour over the pork. Cover tightly and refrigerate 1–8 hours. In a large serving bowl, combine the ginger, cinnamon, marmalade, peaches, onion and parsley. Toss lightly and refrigerate.

Set the Temperature to 350ºF/170ºC and allow the grill to preheat. Place the tenderloins in the grill and set the Timer to 6 minutes for medium, or continue grilling according to your preference. To serve, spoon the salsa over the tenderloins/ filets.

SERVES 4.

NUTRITIONAL ANALYSIS: Calories: **278**   Total fat: **7g**   Saturated fat: **2g**   % calories from fat: **23**   Carbohydrates: **20 g**   Protein: **37 g**   Cholesterol: **101 mg**   Sodium: **586 mg**

Dijon Grilled Pork Tenderloin

A lively Dijon mustard sauce spices up the mild flavor of pork.

4	**6 oz.**/170 g. **pork tenderloin/filets**
2	**cloves garlic, finely minced**
1 T./15 ml.	**Dijon mustard**
1 t./5 g.	**ground ginger**
3 T./45 ml.	**lemon juice**
1 T./15 ml.	**extra virgin olive oil**
1 t./5 g.	**black pepper**
1/2 t./2.5 g.	**salt**

Remove any visible fat from the pork. Set the Temperature to 350ºF/170ºC and allow the grill to preheat. In a small bowl, combine the garlic, mustard, ginger, lemon juice, oil, pepper and salt.

Place the pork in the grill and generously brush with the Dijon mustard sauce. Set the Timer for 6 minutes for medium, or continue grilling if desired.

SERVES 4.

LOW CARB

NUTRITIONAL ANALYSIS: Calories: **252**   Total fat: **10g**   Saturated fat: **3g**
% calories from fat: **36**   Carbohydrates: **3 g**   Protein: **36 g**   Cholesterol: **101 mg**   Sodium: **458 mg**

Pineapple Marinated Pork

Sweet and juicy!

4	**8 oz.**/225 g. **pork tenderloin/filets**
2 c./475 ml.	**unsweetened pineapple juice**
1 t./5 g.	**ground cinnamon**
1 t./5 g.	**ground ginger**
1/2 t./2.5 g.	**salt**
4	**fresh pineapple slices, 1/2-inch**/12 mm **thick (or 4 canned pineapple slices)**
2 oz./55 g.	**slivered almond pieces**
2 T./28 g.	**fresh cilantro/coriander leaves, chopped**

Remove any visible fat from the pork and place the pork in a flat glass pan. Combine the pineapple juice, cinnamon, ginger and salt and pour over the pork. Cover tightly and refrigerate for 2–12 hours.

Set the Temperature to 350ºF/170ºC and allow the grill to preheat. Place the pork in the grill and set the Timer to 3 minutes. When the Timer beeps, place 1 slice of pineapple over each tenderloin/filet. Grill for an additional 2–3 minutes, or according to your preference. Garnish each tenderloin/filet with slivered almonds and cilantro/coriander leaves before serving.

SERVES 4.

NUTRITIONAL ANALYSIS: Calories: **453**   Total fat: **16g**   Saturated fat: **4g**   % calories from fat: **32**   Carbohydrates: **25 g**   Protein: **51 g**   Cholesterol: **134 mg**   Sodium: **388 mg**

Sausage & Herb Stuffed Pork

A perfect Sunday dinner entrée.

4	**6–8 oz.**/170-225 g. **pork tenderloins/filets**
1/2 lb./225 g.	**lowfat sausage/bangers, uncooked, casings removed**
1/2 c./115 g.	**fresh breadcrumbs**
2 T./28 g.	**fresh parsley, minced**
1/2 t./2.5 g.	**ground thyme**
1/2 t./2.5 g.	**ground marjoram**
1 t./5 g.	**black pepper, coarsely ground**

Remove any visible fat from the pork. In a medium mixing bowl, combine the sausage/bangers, breadcrumbs, parsley, thyme, marjoram and pepper. With a sharp knife, cut a slit sideways almost completely through each tenderloin/filet to create a pocket. Open the tenderloins/filets and place one fourth of the sausage/bangers stuffing inside each. Press the edges of the pockets to close.

Set the Temperature to 350ºF/170ºC and allow the grill to preheat. Place the tenderloins/filets in the grill and set the Timer for 5 minutes. Grill until the pork and stuffing are completely cooked. With the plastic spatula, carefully scoop the pork from the grill.

SERVES 4.

NUTRITIONAL ANALYSIS: Calories: **366** Total fat: **11g** Saturated fat: **3g**
% calories from fat: **29** Carbohydrates: **14 g** Protein: **49 g** Cholesterol: **141 mg** Sodium: **446 mg**

Quick & Easy Pork Tenderloins

A 15-minute entrée from start to finish!

4	**6 oz.**/170 g. **pork tenderloins/filets**
1/4 c./60 ml.	**low sodium soy sauce**
2 t./10 g.	**ground ginger**
4	**green/spring onions, chopped**
1	**clove garlic, chopped**
1/2 t./2.5 g.	**black pepper**

Remove all visible fat from the pork. Combine the soy sauce, ginger, onions, garlic and pepper in a flat glass pan. Set the Temperature to 350ºF/170ºC and allow the grill to preheat. Quickly dip each tenderloin/filet into the soy ginger sauce and place in the grill.

Spoon 1 tablespoon/15 ml. of sauce over each tenderloin/filet. Set the Timer to 6 minutes for medium, or continue grilling according to your preference.

SERVES 4.

NUTRITIONAL ANALYSIS: Calories: **227**   Total fat: **6g**   Saturated fat: **2g**
% calories from fat: **26**   Carbohydrates: **3 g**   Protein: **37 g**   Cholesterol: **101 mg**   Sodium: **607 mg**

Caribbean Jerk Pork

The Islands come to your door!

1 lb./450 g.	**pork tenderloin/filet**
1 T./14 g.	**fresh ginger, grated**
1 t./5 g.	**black pepper, coarsely ground**
1 T./14 g.	**brown sugar**
2	**cloves garlic, finely minced**
2 T./28 g.	**fresh cilantro/coriander leaves, chopped**
1/2 t./2.5 g.	**cayenne pepper**
1/4 t./1 g.	**ground nutmeg**
1/4 t./1 g.	**ground coriander**

Remove all visible fat from the pork and place the tenderloin/filet in a flat glass pan. In a small bowl, mix the ginger, pepper, brown sugar, garlic, cilantro/coriander leaves, cayenne pepper, nutmeg and coriander. Blend well to make a thick rub. Press the rub firmly onto all sides of the pork and cover tightly. Refrigerate for 1–2 hours.

Set the Temperature to 350ºF/170ºC to allow the grill to preheat. Place the pork in the grill and set the Timer to 6 minutes for medium. Continue grilling according to your preference. To serve, slice thinly across the grain of the meat.

SERVES 4.

LOW CARB

NUTRITIONAL ANALYSIS: Calories: **154**   Total fat: **4g**   Saturated fat: **1g**
% calories from fat: **26**   Carbohydrates: **4 g**   Protein: **24 g**   Cholesterol: **67 mg**   Sodium: **49 mg**

Grilled Pork with Barbeque Table Mop

These barbequed pork slices are served with a generous "mop," or dipping sauce, at the table.
You may also serve these pork slices on toasted buns for lunch or a football game snack.

1 lb./450 g.	**pork tenderloin/filet**
1 t./5 g.	**salt**
1/2 t./2.5 g.	**black pepper**
8 oz./235 ml.	**low sodium tomato sauce**
2 T./30 ml.	**prepared yellow mustard**
1/2 t./1 ml.	**Tabasco sauce**
1 T./14 g.	**brown sugar**
1	**clove garlic, finely minced**
1	**small white onion, finely chopped**

Remove any visible fat from the pork and dust the tenderloin/filet with the salt and pepper. In a small saucepan, combine the tomato sauce, mustard, Tabasco, brown sugar, garlic and onion and simmer for 20 minutes. Do not boil.

Set the Temperature to 350ºF/170ºC to allow the grill to preheat. Place the tenderloin/filet in the grill and set the Timer for 4 minutes. When the Timer beeps, generously "mop" the pork with the sauce. Continue grilling for 2–4 minutes. Watch the drip tray carefully, as the sauce will melt and run into the tray. To serve, slice thinly across the grain of the meat, heap pork slices on individual plates and cover with additional warm barbeque sauce. **SERVES 4.**

NUTRITIONAL ANALYSIS: Calories: **198** Total fat: **5g** Saturated fat: **1g** % calories from fat: **23** Carbohydrates: **12 g** Protein: **26 g** Cholesterol: **67 mg** Sodium: **641 mg**

Hungarian Paprika Pork Chops

Sweet paprika adds to the spicy rub for these chops.

4	**6 oz.**/170 g. **pork loin chops**
1 t./5 g.	**ground paprika**
1/2 t./2.5 g.	**salt**
1/2 t./2.5 g.	**black pepper**
1/4 t./1 g.	**ground ginger**
1 t./5 g.	**garlic powder**
1/4 t./1 g.	**dry mustard**

Remove all visible fat from the chops. Combine the paprika, salt, pepper, ginger, garlic powder and mustard and rub onto all sides of each chop.

Set the Temperature to 350ºF/170ºC to allow the grill to preheat. Place the chops in the grill and set the Timer for 5 minutes. Grill until medium, or according to your preference.

SERVES 4.

NUTRITIONAL ANALYSIS: Calories: **234**   Total fat: **8g**   Saturated fat: **3g**
% calories from fat: **32**   Carbohydrates: **1 g**   Protein: **37 g**   Cholesterol: **108 mg**   Sodium: **357 mg**

Herbed Pork Chops & New Potatoes

This well-seasoned combination of pork and potatoes is marinated overnight.

4	**4–6 oz.**/120-170 g. **center cut pork chops**
1 lb./450 g.	**small red potatoes**
1 c./250 ml.	**nonfat chicken broth/stock**
1 t./5 g.	**dried rosemary, crumbled**
1/2 t./2.5 g.	**dried marjoram, crumbled**
1/2 t./2.5 g.	**dried sage, crumbled**
1 t./5 g.	**salt**
1 t./5 g.	**black pepper**
1 T./15 ml.	**cider vinegar**

Remove any visible fat from the chops. Place the chops in a flat glass pan. Scrub the potatoes, cut into wedges and put in a self-sealing plastic bag. Mix together in a medium bowl the broth/stock, rosemary, marjoram, sage, salt, pepper and vinegar. Pour one-half of the marinade over the chops and pour the remaining marinade into the plastic bag with the potatoes. Cover the chops tightly, seal the plastic bag and refrigerate both containers overnight.

Set the Temperature to 350ºF/170ºC and allow the grill to preheat. Place the potatoes in the grill and set the Timer to 4 minutes. When the Timer beeps, push the potatoes to the sides of the grill and add the chops. Close the grill and set the Timer for 5 minutes. When the Timer beeps, check the pork and continue grilling for 1 to 2 minutes, if needed. **SERVES 4.**

NUTRITIONAL ANALYSIS: Calories: **216**   Total fat: **5g**   Saturated fat: **2g**
% calories from fat: **21**   Carbohydrates: **21 g**   Protein: **21 g**   Cholesterol: **50 mg**   Sodium: **666 mg**

Texas Barbeque Pork Chops

Always a favorite!

4	**4–6 oz.**/120-170 g. **center cut pork chops**
1/2 t./2.5 g.	**black pepper**
1/2 c./115 g.	**dark brown sugar**
3/4 c./180 ml.	**ketchup**
1	**yellow/strong onion, chopped**
3	**cloves garlic, finely chopped**
1 t./5 g.	**chili powder**

Remove all visible fat from the chops. In a small saucepan, combine the pepper, brown sugar, ketchup, onion, garlic and chili powder. Simmer for 15 minutes until slightly thickened.

Set the Temperature to 350ºF/170ºC to allow the grill to preheat. Place the chops in the grill and spoon 1 heaping tablespoon/20 ml. of sauce over each chop. Set the Timer to 5 minutes and close the grill. When the Timer beeps, add more sauce to each chop and continue grilling if desired. Serve the cooked chops with the remaining warm sauce.

SERVES 4.

NUTRITIONAL ANALYSIS: Calories: **235**   Total fat: **5g**   Saturated fat: **2g**
% calories from fat: **19**   Carbohydrates: **30 g**   Protein: **19 g**   Cholesterol: **50 mg**   Sodium: **414 mg**

Dijon Butter Pork Chops

Dijon mustard butter adds a subtle, tangy flavor to the meat.

4	**6 oz./**170 g. **shoulder pork chops**
1/4 c./55 g.	**lowfat margarine**
1 T./15 ml.	**Dijon mustard**
1 t./5 ml.	**lemon juice**
1 t./5 g.	**fresh parsley, minced**
1 T./14 g.	**green/spring onions, minced**
1/4 t./1 g.	**ground paprika**
1/2 t./2.5 g.	**salt**
1/2 t./2.5 g.	**white pepper**

Remove any visible fat from the chops. In a small bowl, combine the margarine, mustard, lemon juice, parsley, onions, paprika, salt and pepper. Blend well. Set the Temperature to 350ºF/170ºC to allow the grill to preheat.

Place the chops in the grill and top each with 1 tablespoon/15 g. of the Dijon butter. Close the grill and set the Timer for 5 minutes. The Dijon butter will melt and run into the drip tray as the chops grill. To serve, assemble the chops on individual plates and pour the melted Dijon-butter over each chop.

SERVES 4.

NUTRITIONAL ANALYSIS: Calories: **357**   Total fat: **18g**   Saturated fat: **5g**
% calories from fat: **45**   Carbohydrates: **2 g**   Protein: **46 g**   Cholesterol: **138 mg**   Sodium: **540 mg**

Chili Rubbed Pork Chops

Sante Fe-style!

4	**4–6 oz.**/120-170 g. **pork loin chops**
2 T./28 g.	**chili powder**
2 T./28 g.	**brown sugar**
1/2 t./2.5 g.	**salt**
1/2 t./2.5 g.	**ground cumin**
1 T./14 g.	**black pepper, coarsely ground**

Remove all visible fat from the chops. Combine the chili powder, brown sugar, salt, cumin and pepper and generously rub onto all sides of each chop.

Set the Temperature to 350ºF/170ºC and allow the grill to preheat. Place the chops in the grill and set the Timer to 5 minutes. When the Timer beeps, check the chops and continue grilling according to your preference.

SERVES 4.

NUTRITIONAL ANALYSIS: Calories: **186**   Total fat: **6g**   Saturated fat: **2g**   % calories from fat: **29**   Carbohydrates: **8 g**   Protein: **25 g**   Cholesterol: **72 mg**   Sodium: **375 mg**

Teriyaki Pork & Rice Bowls

A quick and delicious dinner-in-a-bowl.

3	**6 oz./170 g. pork loin chops**
2	**green/spring onions, finely chopped**
1/2 c./120 ml.	**low sodium soy sauce**
1 t./5 g.	**ground ginger**
2 T./28 g.	**brown sugar**
2 T./30 ml.	**rice vinegar**
1	**clove garlic, minced**
2 c./450 g.	**cooked long-grain white rice**

Remove any visible fat and the bone from the chops. Cut the pork into very thin slices and set aside. In a small saucepan, heat and blend the onions, soy sauce, ginger, brown sugar, vinegar and garlic to make the teriyaki sauce. Set the Temperature to 350°F/170°C and allow the grill to preheat. Place the pork slices in the grill and set the Timer to 3 minutes. Close the grill.

When the Timer beeps, drizzle 2 tablespoons/30 ml. of sauce over the pork. Spoon the rice over the pork and pour the remaining sauce over the rice. The teriyaki sauce may melt and run into the drip tray.

Lower the Temperature to 325°F/155°C and set the Timer to 2–3 minutes. Close the grill. When the Timer beeps, remove the pork and rice from the grill and serve in individual bowls, spooning any melted sauce over each.

SERVES 4.

NUTRITIONAL ANALYSIS: Calories: **276**   Calories: **6**   Total fats: **6g**   Saturated fat: **2g**   % calories from fat: **20**   Carbohydrates: **23g**   Protein: **31g**   Cholerstorol: **81mg**   Sodium: **765mg**

PORK RIBS, SAUSAGE & HAM
New Orleans Pork Ribs

These boneless ribs take less time and effort to prepare than traditional ribs.

1 1/2 lb./680 g.	**boneless, country-style, pork ribs**
1/4 c./55 g.	**tomato paste**
1/4 c./60 ml.	**cider vinegar**
2 T./28 g.	**honey**
2 T./30 ml.	**water**
1 T./15 ml.	**extra virgin olive oil**
2 t./10 g.	**dry mustard**
1/2 t./2.5 ml.	**Tabasco sauce**
1	**clove garlic, minced**
1/4 c./55 g.	**yellow/strong onion, chopped**

Remove any visible fat from the ribs. Score the ribs with a knife to prevent the meat from curling as it grills. In a small saucepan, combine the remaining ingredients and blend until thickened, about 5 minutes, and keep warm.

Set the Temperature to 350ºF/170ºC to allow the grill to preheat. Place the ribs in the grill and cover each with 1 tablespoon/15 ml. of sauce. Set the Timer for 6 minutes. Grill until the Timer beeps. Open the grill, turn the ribs and baste each with 1 tablespoon/15 ml. of sauce. Grill for 2–4 minutes, or until cooked through. Serve with the remaining warm sauce.

SERVES 4.

NUTRITIONAL ANALYSIS: Calories: **401**   Total fat: **21g**   Saturated fat: **7g**
% calories from fat: **48**   Carbohydrates: **17 g**   Protein: **36 g**   Cholesterol: **110 mg**   Sodium: **105 mg**

Sweet 'n' Smoky Ribs

A tempting favorite Southern recipe.

4 lbs/1.8 kg.	pork baby back ribs/rib part of loin chop
2 T./30 ml.	liquid hickory smoke/barbecue flavoring
1/2 t./2.5 g.	black pepper
1/2 t./2.5 g.	salt
1	clove garlic, minced
2 T./30 ml.	extra virgin olive oil
1/4 c./55 g.	ketchup
1 T./15 ml.	cider vinegar
1 T./14 g.	sugar
1/4 c./60 ml.	orange juice

Slice the ribs into individual pieces. Parboil/steam the ribs for 20 minutes. (To parboil ribs: cook the ribs for 20 minutes in a steamer rack over a pan of boiling water). Cool and remove any visible fat. Place the ribs in a flat glass pan. Combine the liquid smoke, pepper, salt, garlic, oil, ketchup, vinegar, sugar and orange juice and pour over the ribs. Cover tightly and refrigerate for 2–8 hours.

Set the Temperature to 350ºF/170ºC to allow the grill to preheat. Discard the marinade and place the ribs in the grill in a single layer. Close the grill and set the Timer for 5 minutes. When the Timer beeps, check the ribs for doneness and continue grilling if needed. Keep the cooked ribs warm on a serving platter while grilling the remaining ribs.

SERVES 6.

NUTRITIONAL ANALYSIS: Calories: **600**   Total fat: **35g**   Saturated fat: **12g**   % calories from fat: **54**   Carbohydrates: **7 g**   Protein: **59 g**   Cholesterol: **195 mg**   Sodium: **458 mg**

Grilled Italian Sausage & Peppers

Choose from a variety of lowfat sausages to make this dish memorable.

2 lbs./910 g.	lowfat Italian pork sausage (or any other lowfat sausage)
2	green peppers, seeded and thinly sliced
1	white onion, thinly sliced
1 t./5 g.	black pepper
1/2 t./2.5 g.	salt

Cut the sausage into 4 portions. Set the Temperature to 350ºF/170ºC to allow the grill to preheat. Place the sausage, peppers and onion in the grill and dust with pepper and salt. Close the grill and set the Timer for 5 minutes. When the Timer beeps, check the sausage and continue grilling if needed.

SERVES 4.

NUTRITIONAL ANALYSIS: Calories: **430**   Total fat: **18g**   Saturated fat: **5g**
% calories from fat: **36**   Carbohydrates: **23 g**   Protein: **48 g**   Cholesterol: **161 mg**   Sodium: **936 mg**

Sausage & Vegetable Mixed Grill

Perfect for a cold winter evening.

4	**baking potatoes**
1	**yellow/strong onion**
1 t./5 g.	**ground oregano**
1/2 t./2.5 g.	**dried Italian seasoning**
1/2 t./2.5 g.	**black pepper**
2 lbs./910 g.	**lowfat pork sausage links/bangers**

Scrub the potatoes and cut into thin wedges. Peel and thinly slice the onion. Set the Temperature to 400ºF/200ºC to allow the grill to preheat. Place the potatoes and onion in the grill and dust with the oregano, Italian seasoning and pepper. Set the Timer for 3 minutes and close the grill.

When the Timer beeps, reduce the Temperature to 350ºF/170ºC and add the sausages/bangers. Close the grill and set the Timer for 5 minutes. When the Timer beeps, check the sausages/bangers and continue grilling if needed.

SERVES 4.

NUTRITIONAL ANALYSIS: Calories: **549**   Total fat: **18g**   Saturated fat: **5g**   % calories from fat: **29**   Carbohydrates: **50 g**   Protein: **50 g**   Cholesterol: **161 mg**   Sodium: **660 mg**

Applesauce Honey Ham

A quick and pleasing family entrée.

2 lbs./910 g.	**lowfat ham steaks, cut into 8 portions**
1/2 c./115 g.	**applesauce, unsweetened**
2 T./28 g.	**clover honey**
1 t./5 g.	**ground ginger**
1/2 t./2.5 g.	**ground cinnamon**

Remove any visible fat from the steaks. In a small bowl, combine the applesauce, honey, ginger and cinnamon. Set the Temperature to 350ºF/170ºC to allow the grill to preheat. Place the ham in the grill and top with the applesauce honey sauce. Close the grill and set the Timer to 3 minutes.

The applesauce honey mixture will melt and run into the drip tray as the ham grills. Watch carefully to make sure the applesauce does not burn. To serve, place the ham on individual plates and top with the melted applesauce.

SERVES 8.

LOW CARB

NUTRITIONAL ANALYSIS: Calories: **142** Total fat: **4g** Saturated fat: **1g** % calories from fat: **27** Carbohydrates: **9 g** Protein: **17 g** Cholesterol: **40 mg** Sodium: **1,216 mg**

TENDER CHOICES FROM THE SEA
—Fish & Shellfish

Fish and shellfish offer a wide variety of flavors and textures—a bounty of delicious tastes, just waiting to be explored! Whether you choose a delicate and tender fillet of sole with a fresh lemon sauce, a thick grilled salmon steak, or spicy jumbo shrimp skewers, fish and shellfish are a delicious way to pack protein and essential nutrients into your diet.

Marinades and sauces work well with fish prepared in the grill. Depending on the type of fish, you can select fruit, tomato, or herb sauces to accompany it. Many types of fish have a firm texture, such as salmon and swordfish, which partner especially well with sauces. One of our favorite recipes in this chapter is *Thai Salmon Steak,* which grills with a crisp, sweet honey-mustard glaze. A perfect combination of tender fish and a tangy accompaniment!

If you've never spent much time preparing fish before, take a quick look at the recipes that follow. You'll find that *The George Foreman® Lean Mean Fat Reducing Grilling Machine* will make it easy for you, as it grills on both sides and evenly distributes the heat. You may want to prepare the nonstick surface of the grill by spraying it with a nonfat cooking spray and watch the drip tray, as the melted sauces and marinades will collect in the tray. Choose from any of the recipes that follow and stand back to receive the compliments!

FISH FILLETS & STEAKS
Pacific Northwest Salmon Steaks

This exquisite honey-dill sauce creates an unforgettable entrée.

1/4 c./55 g.	clover honey
2 t./10 g.	fresh dill, finely minced
2 t./10 g.	fresh parsley, finely minced
1 T./14 g.	lowfat butter
1/4 t./1 g.	salt
4	6 oz./170 g.	salmon steaks

In a small saucepan, heat the honey, dill, parsley, butter and salt until simmering. Set the Temperature to 300ºF/140ºC to allow the grill to preheat. Place the salmon steaks in the grill and set the Timer to 4 minutes.

When the Timer beeps, spoon the honey-dill sauce over each steak and continue grilling for 2–4 minutes. As the sauce melts, it may run into the drip tray. To serve, drizzle any melted sauce from the tray over the steaks.

SERVES 4.

NUTRITIONAL ANALYSIS: Calories: **442**   Total fat: **22g**   Saturated fat: **5g**
% calories from fat: **46**   Carbohydrates: **18 g**   Protein: **41 g**   Cholesterol: **107 mg**   Sodium: **288 mg**

Spicy Citrus Tuna

Choose very fresh Ahi tuna and grill to medium-rare for best results.

4	**6 oz.**/170 g. **Ahi tuna steaks**
1/2 c./120 ml.	**unsweetened pineapple juice**
1/2 c./120 ml.	**unsweetened orange juice**
1/2 c./120 ml.	**unsweetened grapefruit juice**
1/2 t./2.5 g.	**salt**
1/2 t./2.5 g.	**black pepper**
2 t./10 g.	**ground paprika**
1/4 t./1 g.	**cayenne pepper**

Place the tuna in a flat glass pan. Combine the pineapple juice, orange juice, grapefruit juice, salt, black pepper, paprika and cayenne pepper in a small bowl and pour over the steaks. Cover the fish tightly and refrigerate for 1–2 hours.

Set the Temperature to 375ºF/185ºC to allow the grill to preheat. Place the tuna in the grill and set the Timer for 4 minutes. When the Timer beeps, check the tuna and continue grilling according to your preference. Discard any unused marinade.

SERVES 4.

NUTRITIONAL ANALYSIS: Calories: **311** Total fat: **5g** Saturated fat: **>1g**
% calories from fat: **15** Carbohydrates: **12 g** Protein: **52 g** Cholesterol: **99 mg** Sodium: **372 mg**

Florentine Tuna

A fresh tomato and spinach pasta accompanies the tuna.

1	bunch fresh spinach
1	ripe tomato, chopped
2 T./30 ml.	extra virgin olive oil
1	clove garlic, finely minced
1 T./14 g.	fresh parsley, finely minced
1 T./15 ml.	cider vinegar
1 t./5 g.	salt
1/2 t./2.5 g.	black pepper, coarsely ground
4	**6–8 oz.**/170-225 g. **tuna steaks**
8 oz./225 g.	vermicelli noodles, cooked and drained

Rinse the spinach greens and steam for 5 minutes on the stove over medium heat. Cool and chop finely. In a medium saucepan, combine the chopped spinach, tomato, oil, garlic, parsley, vinegar, salt and pepper. Simmer for 10 minutes.

Set the Temperature to 375ºF/185ºC to allow the grill to preheat. Place the tuna in the grill and set the Timer to 4 minutes. Check the tuna when the Timer beeps and continue grilling if needed. Divide the vermicelli among four individual plates, spoon the sauce over each and top with the grilled tuna.

SERVES 4.

NUTRITIONAL ANALYSIS: Calories: **432**   Total fat: **12g**   Saturated fat: **2g**
% calories from fat: **26**   Carbohydrates: **22 g**   Protein: **57 g**   Cholesterol: **99 mg**   Sodium: **732 mg**

Cajun Rubbed Red Snapper

Snapper has a mild, subtle flavor that makes it a perfect partner for this lively Cajun rub.

1/2 t./2.5 g.	**ground paprika**
1/2 t./2.5 g.	**cayenne pepper**
1/4 t./1 g.	**salt**
1/4 t./1 g.	**black pepper**
1/4 t./1 g.	**garlic powder**
1/4 t./1 g.	**onion powder**
1 T./14 g.	**fresh parsley, finely minced**
4	**6 oz.**/170 g. **red snapper fillets**

In a small plastic bag, mix the paprika, cayenne pepper, salt, black pepper, garlic powder, onion powder and parsley. Shake well and pour onto a plate. Press the fillets into the rub and turn to cover thoroughly.

Set the Temperature to 300ºF/140ºC to allow the grill to preheat. Place the fish in the grill and set the Timer for 3 minutes. When the Timer beeps, check the fish and continue grilling if needed.

SERVES 4.

NUTRITIONAL ANALYSIS: Calories: **248**   Total fat: **6g**   Saturated fat: **>1g**
% calories from fat: **22**   Carbohydrates: **1 g**   Protein: **45 g**   Cholesterol: **80 mg**   Sodium: **243 mg**

Santa Fe Sea Bass

Fresh garden vegetables bring out the best of sea bass.

1/2	green pepper, seeded, diced
1/2	red pepper, seeded, diced
1/2	yellow pepper, seeded, diced
1/2	small white onion, diced
1/2 c./115 g.	cooked corn/sweetcorn
1 T./15 ml.	lime juice
1 T./15 ml.	lemon juice
1 t./5 ml.	extra virgin olive oil
1 t./5 g.	black pepper, coarsely ground
1/2 t./2.5 g.	salt
4	**6 oz.**/170 g. **sea bass fillets**

In a medium bowl, combine the peppers, onion, corn, lime juice, lemon juice, oil, pepper and salt, mixing the vegetables with the seasonings.

Set the Temperature to 300ºF/140ºC and allow the grill to preheat. Place the vegetables in the grill and set the Timer for 3 minutes. When the Timer beeps, add the sea bass fillets to the vegetables, placing the vegetables around the fish in the grill.

Set the Timer for 2 minutes or grill until the fish flakes easily and the vegetables are tender-crisp.

SERVES 4.

NUTRITIONAL ANALYSIS: Calories: **282** Total fat: **9g** Saturated fat: **2g**
% calories from fat: **28** Carbohydrates: **9 g** Protein: **41 g** Cholesterol: **90 mg** Sodium: **152 mg**

LOW CARB

Thai Salmon Steaks

Wonderfully vibrant, tangy flavors!

1 t./5 ml.	**rice vinegar**
2 T./30 ml.	**low sodium soy sauce**
1/4 c./55 g.	**honey**
2 T./30 ml.	**prepared Chinese mustard**
2 T./28 g.	**fresh parsley, finely minced**
4	**6 oz.**/ 170 g. **salmon steaks**

In a small saucepan, combine the vinegar, soy sauce, honey, mustard and parsley. Simmer for 5 minutes.

Set the Temperature to 300ºF/140ºC to allow the grill to preheat. Place the steaks in the grill and cover each with a spoonful of the Thai sauce. Close the grill and set the Timer for 6 minutes. When the Timer beeps, check the salmon and continue grilling if needed. Serve with any remaining sauce.

SERVES 4.

NUTRITIONAL ANALYSIS: Calories: **401**   Total fat: **17g**   Saturated fat: **4g**
% calories from fat: **39**   Carbohydrates: **19 g**   Protein: **42 g**   Cholesterol: **107 mg**   Sodium: **454 mg**

Lemon Basil Halibut

A healthful and elegant entrée for a casual dinner party.

4	**6 oz.**/170 g. **halibut steaks**
1 t./5 g.	**ground paprika**
1/2 c./115 g.	**lowfat margarine**
1 T./14 g.	**fresh basil, finely minced**
1 T./15 ml.	**lemon juice**
1 T./14 g.	**green/spring onion, finely minced**

Set the Temperature to 300ºF/140ºC to allow the grill to preheat. Place the steaks in the grill and sprinkle with the paprika. Close the grill and set the Timer to 6 minutes. When the Timer beeps, check the fish and continue grilling if needed.

In a small bowl, blend the margarine, basil, lemon juice and onion. To serve, arrange each steak on a plate and top with a generous spoonful of the lemon-basil butter.

SERVES 4.

NUTRITIONAL ANALYSIS: Calories: **325** Total fat: **11g** Saturated fat: **2g**
% calories from fat: **33** Carbohydrates: **4 g** Protein: **46 g** Cholesterol: **70 mg** Sodium: **271 mg**

Grilled Swordfish with Fresh Tomato Herb Couli

A smooth sauce of tomato and herbs accents the swordfish.

1 t./5 ml.	extra virgin olive oil
1 T./15 ml.	lemon juice
3	ripe tomatoes, chopped
1/4 c./60 ml.	canned tomato sauce
3 T./42 g.	white onion, chopped
1/2 c./115 g.	fresh bread crumbs
1/2 t./2.5 g.	ground oregano
1/4 t./1 g.	dried rosemary
1/2 t./2.5 g.	salt
1/2 t./2.5 g.	black pepper
4	8 oz./225 g. **swordfish steaks**

Place all of the ingredients except the swordfish steaks in a blender and pulse until smooth. Let stand up to 1 hour until ready to use.

Set the Temperature to 375ºF/185ºC and allow the grill to preheat. Place the swordfish in the grill and set the Timer for 6 minutes. When the Timer beeps, check the fish and continue grilling if needed. To serve, pour the sauce equally onto four plates and top with the grilled swordfish.

SERVES 4.

NUTRITIONAL ANALYSIS: Calories: **295**   Total fat: **11g**   Saturated fat: **2g**
% calories from fat: **34**   Carbohydrates: **15 g**   Protein: **34 g**   Cholesterol: **60 mg**   Sodium: **633 mg**

Quick & Easy Halibut Fillets

The perfect answer to a busy day.

1 t./5 ml.	**extra virgin olive oil**
2 T./30 ml.	**lemon juice**
1	**clove garlic, finely minced**
1 T./14 g.	**fresh parsley, finely minced**
1 t./5 g.	**black pepper, coarsely ground**
4	**6 oz.**/170 g. **halibut fillets**

In a small bowl, combine the oil, lemon juice, garlic, parsley and black pepper.

Set the Temperature to 300ºF/140ºC to allow the grill to preheat. Place the fillets in the grill, drizzle the lemon sauce over each and set the Timer for 4 minutes. When the Timer beeps, check the fish and continue grilling if needed.

SERVES 4.

NUTRITIONAL ANALYSIS: Calories: **280**   Total fat: **9g**   Saturated fat: **1g**
% calories from fat: **30**   Carbohydrates: **2 g**   Protein: **46 g**   Cholesterol: **70 mg**   Sodium: **118 mg**

Orange Pressed Tuna

The sweet juice of the orange grills into the tuna.

4	**6 oz.**/170 g. **Ahi tuna steaks**
1	**fresh sweet orange**
1 t./5 g.	**fresh parsley, finely minced**
1/2 t./2.5 g.	**salt**
1/4 t./1 g.	**black pepper**

Peel and slice the orange into 1⁄4-inch/6 mm thick slices. Set the Temperature to 375ºF/185ºC to allow the grill to preheat. Place the tuna in the grill and sprinkle the parsley, salt and pepper over each steak. Cover with the orange slices.

Close the grill and set the Timer to 4 minutes. When the Timer beeps, check the tuna and continue grilling if preferred. Discard the grilled orange slices and serve.

SERVES 4.

NUTRITIONAL ANALYSIS: Calories: **279**   Total fat: **5g**   Saturated fat: **>1g**
% calories from fat: **17**   Carbohydrates: **4 g**   Protein: **51 g**   Cholesterol: **99 mg**   Sodium: **371 mg**

Orange Roughy Primavera

Orange roughy is sweet, mild and very delicate.

1	**zucchini/courgette, cleaned**
1	**red pepper, cleaned**
1	**yellow/strong onion**
1	**carrot, peeled**
1 t./5 g.	**fresh rosemary, minced**
1 t./5 g.	**fresh thyme, minced**
1 t./5 g.	**black pepper, coarsely ground**
1 t./5 ml.	**extra virgin olive oil**
4	**6 oz.**/170 g. **orange roughy fillets**

Thinly slice the zucchini/courgette, red pepper, onion and carrot. In a small bowl, combine the rosemary, thyme, pepper and oil. Set the Temperature to 325ºF/155ºC to allow the grill to preheat. Place the vegetables in the grill and drizzle one half of the herb oil over them. Close the grill and set the Timer for 5 minutes.

When the Timer beeps, move the vegetables to the sides of the grill and add the fillets. Drizzle the remaining herb oil over the fillets. Set the Temperature to 300ºF/140ºC and close the grill. Set the Timer for 3 minutes.

When the Timer beeps, check the fish and continue grilling, if needed, until the fish flakes easily and the vegetables are tender. To serve, carefully remove the fillets from the grill and top with the vegetables. **SERVES 4.**

NUTRITIONAL ANALYSIS: Calories: **223**   Total fat: **6g**   Saturated fat: **>1g**   % calories from fat: **23**   Carbohydrates: **8 g**   Protein: **34 g**   Cholesterol: **44 mg**   Sodium: **150 mg**

LOW CARB

Halibut with Avocado Lemon Cream

The creamy flavor of avocados makes this halibut memorable!

1	**Haas avocado**
1 T./15 ml.	**lemon juice**
1/2 c./115 g.	**nonfat cream cheese**
4	**6 oz.**/170 g. **halibut steaks**
1 t./5 g.	**black pepper, coarsely ground**
1 t./5 g.	**salt**
1 T./15 ml.	**lemon juice**

In a small bowl, peel and mash the avocado until smooth. Stir in the lemon juice and cream cheese and blend thoroughly. Refrigerate.

Set the Temperature to 300ºF/140ºC to allow the grill to preheat. Place the halibut in the grill and sprinkle with the pepper, salt and lemon juice. Close the grill and set the Timer for 6 minutes. When the Timer beeps, check the fish and continue grilling if needed. To serve, top each fillet with one-fourth of the avocado cream.

SERVES 4.

NUTRITIONAL ANALYSIS: Calories: **374**   Total fat: **15g**   Saturated fat: **2g**
% calories from fat: **38**   Carbohydrates: **9 g**   Protein: **49 g**   Cholesterol: **70 mg**   Sodium: **734 mg**

Grilled Oriental Tuna

Serve rare to medium rare for best results.

2 T./30 ml.	**low sodium soy sauce**
1/4 c./60 ml.	**Asian hoisin sauce**
1 t./5 g.	**honey**
1 t./5 ml.	**sesame oil**
1 t./5 ml.	**Szechuan chile sauce**
4	**6 oz.**/170 g. **Ahi tuna steaks**

In a small bowl, combine the soy sauce, hoisin sauce, honey, sesame oil and chile sauce. Place the tuna in a flat glass pan and spoon the sauce over each steak. Refrigerate, covered, for 1 hour.

Set the Temperature to 375ºF/185ºC and allow the grill to preheat. Place the steaks in the grill and set the Timer to 4 minutes. When the Timer beeps, check the steaks and continue grilling according to your preference.

SERVES 4.

NUTRITIONAL ANALYSIS: Calories: **320**   Total fat: **7g**   Saturated fat: **1g**
% calories from fat: **19**   Carbohydrates: **10 g**   Protein: **52 g**   Cholesterol: **99 mg**   Sodium: **872**

Italian Rubbed Sea Bass Fillets

From the shores of Southern Italy.

2 t./10 g.	**chili powder**
1 T./14 g.	**ground paprika**
1	**clove garlic, finely minced**
1/4 c./55 g.	**fresh cilantro/coriander leaves, finely minced**
1/2 t./2.5 g.	**black pepper, coarsely ground**
1 t./5 g.	**salt**
4	**6 oz.**/170 g. **sea bass fillets**

In a small plastic bag, mix together the chili powder, paprika, garlic, cilantro/coriander leaves, pepper and salt. Shake well and pour onto a plate. Place each fillet on the plate and press lightly to absorb the spices.

Set the Temperature 300ºF/140ºC to allow the grill to preheat. Place the fillets in the grill and set the Timer to 3 minutes. When the Timer beeps, check the fillets and continue grilling if needed.

SERVES 4.

NUTRITIONAL ANALYSIS: Calories: **249**   Total fat: **8g**   Saturated fat: **1g**
% calories from fat: **28**   Carbohydrates: **3 g**   Protein: **41 g**   Cholesterol: **90 mg**   Sodium: **744 mg**

Mango Orange Mahi-Mahi

For a very special occasion.

3 c./680 g.	**mangos, chopped**
2	**green/spring onions, finely chopped**
1 T./14 g.	**fresh parsley, finely minced**
3 T./45 ml.	**orange juice**
4	**6–7 oz.**/170-200 g. **mahi-mahi fillets**

In a medium bowl, combine the mangos, onions, parsley and orange juice. Refrigerate.

Set the Temperature to 300ºF/140ºC to allow the grill to preheat. Place the mahi-mahi in the grill and set the Timer to 3 minutes. When the Timer beeps, check the fish and continue grilling if needed.

Divide the mango salsa into 4 equal portions and serve on top of the fish.

SERVES 4.

NUTRITIONAL ANALYSIS: Calories: **261**   Total fat: **4g**   Saturated fat: **>1g**
% calories from fat: **15**   Carbohydrates: **24 g**   Protein: **32 g**   Cholesterol: **124 mg**   Sodium: **153 mg**

SHELLFISH
Cilantro Lime-Dipped Shrimp

Grilled to perfection with just a hint of Mexican spices.

2 t./10 ml.	**extra virgin olive oil**
1/4 c./60 ml.	**lime juice**
2 T./28 g.	**fresh cilantro/coriander leaves, finely chopped**
1/4 t./1 g.	**cayenne pepper**
1/2 t./2.5 g.	**salt**
1/2 t./2.5 g.	**black pepper**
16	**jumbo uncooked shrimp, peeled, deveined, tails removed**
4	**8-inch**/20 cm **wooden skewers, soaked in water and drained**

Mix the oil, lime juice, cilantro/coriander leaves, cayenne pepper, salt and pepper to make a marinade. Place the shrimp in the marinade and refrigerate for 1–2 hours.

Set the Temperature to 300ºF/140ºC to allow the grill to preheat. Discard the marinade. Arrange 4 shrimp on each skewer and place in the grill widthwise (horizontally). Close the grill and set the Timer for 2 minutes. When the Timer beeps, check the shrimp and continue grilling if needed.

SERVES 4.

NUTRITIONAL ANALYSIS: Calories: 77   Total fat: 5g   Saturated fat: >1g
% calories from fat: 62   Carbohydrates: 2 g   Protein: 5 g   Cholesterol: 47 mg   Sodium: 345 mg

Vietnamese Lettuce-Wrapped Shrimp

This simple dish uses shrimp sparingly, but doesn't skimp on flavor.

16	large uncooked shrimp, peeled, deveined, tails removed
1/2 t./1 ml.	Asian chile oil
1/4 t./1 g.	black pepper
1 T./15 ml.	sesame oil
1 T./15 ml.	low sodium soy sauce
24	leaves of butter lettuce, rinsed
2 c./450 g.	carrots, peeled and grated
2 c./450 g.	bean sprouts, rinsed and cut into 1-inch/2.5 cm pieces
1/4 c./60 ml.	hoisin sauce
4	8-inch/20 cm wooden skewers, soaked in water and drained

Thread the shrimp onto the skewers. Combine the chile oil, pepper, sesame oil and soy sauce. Set the Temperature to 300ºF/140ºC to allow the grill to preheat. Place the skewers in the grill widthwise (horizontally) and brush with the sauce. Close the grill and set the Timer for 2 minutes. When the Timer beeps, check the shrimp and continue grilling if needed. To assemble, place shrimp, carrots and bean sprouts on individual lettuce leaves. Tuck in the ends and roll. Dip the lettuce wraps in the hoisin sauce as desired. **SERVES 4.**

NUTRITIONAL ANALYSIS: Calories: **169**   Total fat: **8g**   Saturated fat: **1g**   % calories from fat: **40**   Carbohydrates: **18 g**   Protein: **9 g**   Cholesterol: **47 mg**   Sodium: **594 mg**

Surf & Sea Kebabs

Pair with creamy risotto for a lovely meal.

12	**large uncooked shrimp, peeled, deveined, tails removed**
1/2 lb./225 g.	**halibut, cut into 1-inch**/2.5 cm **cubes**
1	**red pepper, cut into 1-inch**/2.5 cm **pieces**
1/2	**purple/red onion, cut into 1-inch**/2.5 cm **pieces**
2 T./28 g.	**lowfat margarine**
1 t./5 g.	**black pepper, coarsely ground**
1 t./5 g.	**seasoned salt**
8	**10-inch**/25 cm **wooden skewers, soaked in water and drained**

Thread the shrimp and halibut with the red pepper and onion onto the skewers, alternating each. In a small bowl, combine the margarine, pepper and seasoned salt.

Set the Temperature to 300ºF/140ºC to allow the grill to preheat. Place the kebabs in the grill widthwise (horizontally) and brush with the seasoned butter. Close the grill and set the Timer for 4 minutes.

When the Timer beeps, check the fish and vegetables and continue grilling for up to 3 minutes, or until the fish flakes easily and the vegetables are tender. As the butter melts, it will run into the drip tray. If desired, you may serve any melted sauce as an accompaniment to the grilled kebabs.

SERVES 4.

LOW CARB

NUTRITIONAL ANALYSIS: Calories: **152** Total fat: **6g** Saturated fat: **>1g** % calories from fat: **34** Carbohydrates: **4 g** Protein: **19 g** Cholesterol: **58 mg** Sodium: **466 mg**

Scallops en Brochette

Serve with steamed spinach and angel hair pasta for an easy meal.

24	**sea scallops**
2 t./10 ml.	**extra virgin olive oil**
2 T./30 ml.	**white vinegar**
1/4 c./60 ml.	**low sodium soy sauce**
1 t./5 g.	**ground ginger**
1	**clove garlic, finely minced**
1 T./14 g.	**fresh parsley, finely minced**
4	**10-inch**/25 cm **wooden skewers, soaked in water and drained**

Clean the scallops and place in a self-sealing plastic bag. Combine the oil, vinegar, soy sauce, ginger, garlic and parsley together and pour over the scallops. Seal the bag and refrigerate 1–3 hours.

Set the Temperature to 300ºF/140ºC to allow the grill to preheat. Discard the marinade. Thread the scallops on the skewers and place in the grill widthwise (horizontally). Close the grill and set the Timer for 3 minutes. When the Timer beeps, check the scallops and continue grilling if needed. Watch carefully to avoid overcooking. Discard any remaining marinade.

<u>**SERVES 4.**</u>

NUTRITIONAL ANALYSIS:	Calories: **95**	Total fat: **4g**	Saturated fat: **>1g**	
% calories from fat: **40**	Carbohydrates: **3 g**	Protein: **11 g**	Cholesterol: **19 mg**	Sodium: **781 mg**

SAVORY GRILLED POULTRY
—Chicken & Turkey

Whether you need a quick dinner for yourself or enough food for friends and family, chances are chicken or turkey will often be found on your menu. Poultry is full of flavor, easy to prepare and enjoyable to eat. And, because individually frozen boneless chicken breasts are so easy to keep on hand, they are the perfect complement to *The George Foreman® Lean Mean Fat Reducing Grilling Machine.* Chicken gets a "two-thumbs-up" review whenever it is grilled and served with herbs, spices, sauces or salsas. Almost any poultry choice is a winner!

Grilling brings out the best of poultry and the recipes that follow have their origins in countries all over the world. You'll find Mexican, Caribbean, Italian, French and Japanese spices and herbs used in these recipes. In addition, we've included some recipes such as *Old Retreat Glazed Chicken Breasts* and *Sage-Stuffed Chicken Breasts* that are a new twist on favorite entrées from the past.

You probably already know that chicken and turkey breast meat are low in fat and high in protein, but you may not know that the skin of both has a high fat content and should be discarded. The recipes in this chapter call for boneless, skinless chicken and turkey meat. You may use frozen or fresh poultry, but be sure to thaw frozen poultry in the refrigerator and safely handle all raw poultry to avoid contamination. Poultry should be completely cooked to 170–180°F/77–82°C and juices should run clear.

Fajita Rubbed Chicken

This grilled chicken makes a delicious start for tacos or fajitas.

1 T./14 g.	chili powder
1/2 t./2.5 g.	cayenne pepper
1 T./14 g.	fresh parsley, minced
1 T./14 g.	brown sugar
1/2 t./2.5 g.	black pepper
1/4 t./1 g.	ground cumin
4	boneless, skinless chicken breast halves

Combine the chili powder, cayenne pepper, parsley, brown sugar, pepper and cumin on a large plate. Mix the spices thoroughly. Press each chicken breast into the spices on all sides.

Set the Temperature to 375°F/185°C to allow the grill to preheat. Place the chicken in the grill and set the Timer to 5 minutes. When the Timer beeps, check the chicken with the tip of a knife. If the chicken is not cooked completely through, continue grilling for 1 to 2 minutes.

SERVES 4.

NUTRITIONAL   ANALYSIS: Calories: **348**   Total   fat: **10g**   Saturated   fat: **2g**
% calories from fat: **26**   Carbohydrates: **7 g**   Protein: **56 g**   Cholesterol: **146 mg**   Sodium: **197 mg**

Dijon Grilled Chicken Breasts

Tangy mustard is the perfect partner for chicken.

1 T./15 ml.	**Dijon mustard**
1 T./15 ml.	**nonfat mayonnaise**
1 t./5 ml.	**cider vinegar**
1 t./5 g.	**black pepper**
1/2 t./2.5 g.	**salt**
1	**clove garlic, minced**
4	**boneless, skinless chicken breast halves**

In a small bowl, mix together the mustard, mayonnaise, vinegar, pepper, salt and garlic. Set aside.

Set the Temperature to 375ºF/185ºC to allow the grill to preheat. Place the chicken in the grill, spoon the sauce over each breast and set the Timer to 5 minutes. When the Timer beeps, check the chicken with the tip of a knife. If the chicken is not cooked completely through, continue grilling for 1 to 2 minutes.

SERVES 4.

LOW CARB

NUTRITIONAL ANALYSIS: Calories: **325** Total fat: **9g** Saturated fat: **2g**
% calories from fat: **26** Carbohydrates: **2 g** Protein: **56 g** Cholesterol: **146 mg** Sodium: **535 mg**

Japanese Soy Chicken

Serve with Japanese stir-fry vegetables and steamed brown rice for a delicious and healthy meal.

1/4 c./60 ml.	low sodium soy sauce
1 t./5 ml.	vegetable oil
1 t./5 ml.	Asian chile oil
1	clove garlic, minced
1 t./5 g.	ground ginger
1/2 t./2.5 g.	black pepper
1 t./5 ml.	clover honey
4	boneless, skinless chicken breast halves

In a flat glass pan, combine the soy sauce, oils, garlic, ginger, pepper and honey. Mix well to dissolve the honey. Add the chicken breasts and turn to coat. Cover and refrigerate 1–4 hours.

Set the Temperature to 375ºF/185ºC to allow the grill to preheat. Discard the marinade. Place the chicken in the grill and set the Timer to 5 minutes. When the Timer beeps, check the chicken with the tip of a knife. If the chicken is not cooked completely through, continue grilling for 1 to 2 minutes.

SERVES 4.

NUTRITIONAL ANALYSIS: Calories: **181**   Total fat: **5g**   Saturated fat: **1g**
% calories from fat: **27**   Carbohydrates: **4 g**   Protein: **28 g**   Cholesterol: **73 mg**   Sodium: **593 mg**

Sweet & Spicy Barbeque Chicken

Divide this sauce—use half for grilling and half as a table sauce.

1	**15 oz.**/425 g.	**can tomato sauce**
2		**cloves garlic, finely minced**
1 t./5 ml.		**extra virgin olive oil**
1		**yellow/strong onion, finely chopped**
2 T./30 ml.		**Worcestershire sauce**
1 t./5 g.		**chili powder**
2 T./30 ml.		**cider vinegar**
4		**boneless, skinless chicken breast halves**

Combine the tomato sauce, garlic, oil, onion, Worcestershire sauce, chili powder and vinegar in a small saucepan. Heat and stir for 5 minutes. Remove 1/2 cup/120 ml. of the sauce and keep the remainder at a warm temperature, but do not boil.

Set the Temperature to 375°F/185°C to allow the grill to preheat. Place the chicken in the grill and spoon 1/2 of the sauce over each breast. Close the grill and set the Timer to 5 minutes. When the Timer beeps, check the chicken with the tip of a knife. If the chicken is not cooked completely through, continue grilling for 1 to 2 minutes. Pass the remaining sauce with the grilled chicken.

SERVES 4.

NUTRITIONAL ANALYSIS: Calories: **238**   Total fat: **7g**   Saturated fat: **1g**
% calories from fat: **27**   Carbohydrates: **14 g**   Protein: **30 g**   Cholesterol: **73 mg**   Sodium: **794 mg**

Tamari Lemon Chicken

*This entrée is easy to prepare and impressive when served. You'll find tamari,
a premium soy sauce, in the specialty food section of the grocery store.*

1 T./15 ml.	tamari soy sauce
1 T./14 g.	fresh parsley, finely minced
2 T./30 ml.	extra virgin olive oil
3 T./45 ml.	lemon juice
1 T./14 g.	black pepper, coarsely ground
6	boneless, skinless chicken breast halves

In a small bowl, combine the tamari, parsley, oil, lemon juice and pepper.

Set the Temperature to 375ºF/185ºC to allow the grill to preheat. Discard
the marinade. Place the chicken in the grill and drizzle with the tamari sauce. Close
the grill and set the Timer to 5 minutes. When the Timer beeps, check the chicken
with the tip of a knife. If the chicken is not cooked completely through, continue
grilling for 1 to 2 minutes.

SERVES 6.

NUTRITIONAL   ANALYSIS: Calories: **207**   Total fat: **7g**   Saturated fat: **1g**
% calories from fat: **18**   Carbohydrates: **2 g**   Protein: **28 g**   Cholesterol: **73 mg**   Sodium: **172 mg**

Jerk Chicken with Cilantro/Coriander Rice

Perfect for a weekend supper.

1/2 c./120 ml.	lemon juice
2 T./30 ml.	Szechuan chili sauce
1 T./14 g.	fresh parsley, minced
2 T./30 ml.	vegetable oil
1 t./5 g.	ground paprika
1 T./15 ml.	prepared yellow mustard
4	boneless, skinless chicken breast halves
2 c./450 g.	long grain rice, cooked
2 T./28 g.	fresh cilantro/coriander leaves, finely chopped
2 T./28 g.	green/spring onion, sliced
1	carrot, peeled and grated

NUTRITIONAL ANALYSIS: Calories: **361** Total fat: **10g** Saturated fat: **2g** % calories from fat: **25** Carbohydrates: **38 g** Protein: **32 g** Cholesterol: **73 mg** Sodium: **194 mg**

Combine the lemon juice, chili sauce, parsley, oil, paprika and mustard in a small bowl. Set the Temperature to 375ºF/185ºC to allow the grill to preheat. Place the chicken breasts in the grill and spoon the jerk sauce over each piece. Close the grill and set the Timer for 5 minutes. Watch the drip tray carefully, as the sauce will melt and run into the tray. When the Timer beeps, check the chicken with the tip of a knife. If the chicken is not cooked completely through, continue grilling for 1 to 2 minutes.

Remove the chicken from the grill and keep warm. In a large bowl, combine the rice, cilantro/coriander leaves, onion and carrot. Set aside.

Lightly coat the grilling plates with nonstick cooking spray. Set the Temperature to 325ºF/155ºC to allow the grill to preheat. Scoop the rice onto the grill and drizzle the melted sauce over the rice. Close the grill and set the Timer to 3 minutes. To serve, arrange the rice on a large platter and top with the chicken breasts.

SERVES 4.

Hoisin-Glazed Chicken Thighs

Sweet and tangy hoisin sauce is readily available in the specialty food section of the grocery store.

8	**boneless, skinless chicken thighs**
1/4 c./60 ml.	**hoisin sauce**
2 T./30 ml.	**prepared barbeque sauce**
1 T./15 ml.	**Worcestershire sauce**
1	**green/spring onion, chopped**

Remove any visible fat from the chicken. Place the thighs in a flat glass pan. Combine the hoisin sauce, barbeque sauce, Worcestershire sauce and onion and pour over the thighs. Cover tightly and refrigerate for 1–8 hours.

Set the Temperature to 375ºF/185ºC to allow the grill to preheat. Discard the marinade. Place the chicken in the grill and set the Timer to 5 minutes. When the Timer beeps, check the chicken with the tip of a knife. If the chicken is not cooked completely through, continue grilling for 1 to 2 minutes.

SERVES 4-6.

LOW CARB

NUTRITIONAL ANALYSIS: Calories: **143**   Total fat: **4g**   Saturated fat: **>1g**
% calories from fat: **27**   Carbohydrates: **7 g**   Protein: **18 g**   Cholesterol: **76 mg**   Sodium: **348 mg**

Indian Coriander Chicken

This chicken is sweet, tender and juicy!

4	**boneless, skinless chicken breast halves**
1/2 c./120 ml.	**lemon juice**
1/4 c./60 ml.	**water**
1 t./5 g.	**black pepper**
1 t./5 g.	**ground coriander**
1/2 t./2.5 g.	**ground cloves**
1/2 t./2.5 g.	**ground bay leaves**
1 t./5 g.	**salt**

Place the chicken in a flat glass pan. In a small bowl, combine the lemon juice, water, pepper, coriander, cloves, bay leaves and salt. Pour the marinade over the chicken, cover tightly and refrigerate for 1–10 hours.

Set the Temperature to 375ºF/185ºC to allow the grill to preheat. Discard the marinade. Place the chicken in the grill and set the Timer to 5 minutes. When the Timer beeps, check the chicken with the tip of a knife. If the chicken is not cooked completely through, continue grilling for 1 to 2 minutes.

SERVES 4.

NUTRITIONAL ANALYSIS: Calories: **183**   Total fat: **4g**   Saturated fat: **1g**
% calories from fat: **29**   Carbohydrates: **4 g**   Protein: **28 g**   Cholesterol: **73 mg**   Sodium: **643 mg**

LOW CARB

Old Retreat Glazed Chicken Breasts

This barbeque glaze holds just a hint of maple syrup for sweetness.

1	**small white onion, finely chopped**
1	**15 oz.**/445 ml. **can tomato sauce**
1 T./15 ml.	**prepared yellow mustard**
2 T./30 ml.	**cider vinegar**
1/4 c./60 ml.	**maple syrup**
1 t./5 ml.	**Worcestershire sauce**
6	**boneless, skinless chicken breast halves**

In a medium saucepan, combine the onion, tomato sauce, mustard, vinegar, maple syrup and Worcestershire sauce. Heat and simmer for 15 minutes.

Set the Temperature to 375ºF/185ºC to allow the grill to preheat. Place the chicken in the grill and spoon 1 tablespoon/15 ml. of the sauce over each piece. Close the grill and set the Timer to 2 minutes. When the Timer beeps, open the grill and spoon the sauce over the chicken again. Close the grill and set the Timer to 3 minutes.

When the Timer beeps, check the chicken with the tip of a knife. If the chicken is not cooked completely through, continue grilling for 1 to 2 minutes. Pass the remaining sauce with the chicken.

SERVES 6.

NUTRITIONAL   ANALYSIS: Calories: **225**   Total fat: **5g**   Saturated fat: **1g**
% calories from fat: **20**   Carbohydrates: **16 g**   Protein: **29 g**   Cholesterol: **73 mg**   Sodium: **531 mg**

Turkey Aglia Olio

A simple Italian farmer's dinner made especially good by adding tender grilled turkey.

1 lb./450 g.	**boneless, skinless turkey breast**
2 T./30 ml.	**extra virgin olive oil**
4	**cloves garlic, finely minced**
2 T./28 g.	**fresh parsley, finely minced**
1 t./5 g.	**ground oregano**
1/4 c./55 g.	**Parmesan cheese, grated**
1 t./5 g.	**black pepper, coarsely ground**
1/2 t./2.5 g.	**salt**
10 oz./285 g.	**angel hair/vermicelli pasta, hot, cooked**

Slice the turkey breast thinly across the grain of the meat. In a small bowl, combine the oil, garlic, parsley, oregano, Parmesan cheese, pepper and salt.

Set the Temperature to 350ºF /170ºC to allow the grill to preheat. Place the turkey slices in the grill and set the Timer to 3 minutes. When the Timer beeps, check the turkey with the tip of a knife. If the turkey is not cooked completely through, continue grilling for 1 to 2 minutes.

To serve, place the pasta on a serving platter, pour the sauce over and toss well. Arrange the turkey slices on top and serve immediately.

SERVES 4.

NUTRITIONAL ANALYSIS: Calories: **349**   Total fat: **13g**   Saturated fat: **3g**
% calories from fat: **34**   Carbohydrates: **20 g**   Protein: **36 g**   Cholesterol: **110 mg**   Sodium: **871 mg**

Orange Ginger Grilled Chicken

A piquant sauce!

1/2 c./120 ml.	**concentrated frozen orange juice**
1 t./5 g.	**ground ginger**
1/4 c./60 ml.	**orange marmalade**
2 T./30 ml.	**water**
1 t./5 g.	**salt**
1/2 t./2.5 g.	**black pepper**
4	**boneless, skinless chicken breast halves**
1	**naval orange, peeled and cut into thin slices**

In a small bowl, combine the juice, ginger, marmalade, water, salt and pepper. Mix well to dissolve the orange juice and marmalade.

Set the Temperature to 375ºF/185ºC to allow the grill to preheat. Place the chicken in the grill and cover each piece with the orange sauce. Close the grill and set the Timer to 5 minutes. When the Timer beeps, check the chicken with the tip of a knife. If the chicken is not cooked completely through, continue grilling for 1 to 2 minutes. To serve, garnish the chicken with the orange slices.

SERVES 4.

NUTRITIONAL ANALYSIS: Calories: **294** Total fat: **6g** Saturated fat: **1g** % calories from fat: **18** Carbohydrates: **52 g** Protein: **29 g** Cholesterol: **73 mg** Sodium: **654 mg**

Sage-Stuffed Chicken Breasts

A new twist on an old favorite.

4	**boneless, skinless chicken breast halves**
1 c./225 g.	**prepared herb stuffing mix, cooled**
2 T./28 g.	**white onion, finely chopped**
1 t./5 g.	**ground sage**
1/2 t./2.5 g.	**dried rosemary**

Place the chicken on a clean cutting surface. With the tip of a sharp knife, slit each breast open horizontally without cutting through the entire breast, to create a pocket. In a medium bowl, toss together the stuffing mix, onion, sage, and rosemary. Stuff one-fourth of the dressing in each chicken breast and press the edges of the chicken breast together to close the pocket. A small bit of stuffing may spill out slightly during grilling, but this will not affect the outcome of the chicken.

Set the Temperature to 375ºF/185ºC to allow the grill to preheat. Place the chicken in the grill and set the Timer to 5 minutes. When the Timer beeps, check the stuffed chicken with the tip of a knife. If the chicken is not cooked completely through, continue grilling for 1 to 2 minutes. Scoop up any excess stuffing with the plastic spatula and serve with the chicken.

SERVES 4.

NUTRITIONAL ANALYSIS: Calories: **416**   Total fat: **13g**   Saturated fat: **3g**
% calories from fat: **29**   Carbohydrates: **14 g**   Protein: **58 g**   Cholesterol: **146 mg**   Sodium: **387 mg**

Chicken & Sausage Mixed Grill

Choose your favorite lowfat sausage for this tasty combination!

1	red pepper, seeded and thinly sliced
1	green pepper, seeded and thinly sliced
1	small white onion, thinly sliced
1 t./5 g.	black pepper
1 t./5 g.	salt
1 T./15 ml.	extra virgin olive oil
1 T./15 ml.	lemon juice
1 lb./450 g.	lowfat link sausage/bangers
4	boneless, skinless chicken breast halves

In a large bowl, mix together the peppers, onion, black pepper, salt, oil and lemon juice. Let stand for 10 minutes to blend the flavors. Cut the chicken breasts into slices approximately the same size as the sausages/bangers.

Set the Temperature to 375ºF/185ºC to allow the grill to preheat. Place the chicken and sausages/bangers in the grill and set the Timer to 2 minutes. When the Timer beeps, place the pepper and onion mixture on top and grill for an additional 3–5 minutes, or until the chicken and sausages/bangers are fully cooked and the vegetables are tender.

SERVES 4.

NUTRITIONAL ANALYSIS: Calories: **417**   Total fat: **18g**   Saturated fat: **4g**   % calories from fat: **39**   Carbohydrates: **13 g**   Protein: **51 g**   Cholesterol: **153 mg**   Sodium: **964 mg**

Tandoori Grilled Chicken

The yogurt-based marinade creates exotic, tender chicken!

8 oz./225 g.	carton unflavored lowfat yogurt
1 T./15 ml.	lemon juice
2 t./10 g.	ground paprika
2	cloves garlic, minced
1/2 t./2.5 g.	salt
1/2 t./2.5 g.	ground ginger
1/2 t./2.5 g.	ground cumin
1/2 t./2.5 g.	cayenne pepper
1/2 t./2.5 g.	ground cinnamon
4	boneless, skinless chicken breast halves

In a small bowl, mix together the yogurt, lemon juice, paprika, garlic, salt, ginger, cumin, cayenne pepper and cinnamon. Place the chicken breasts in a shallow glass pan and pour the marinade over the pieces, turning to coat thoroughly. Cover tightly and refrigerate for 1–8 hours, turning occasionally.

Set the Temperature to 375ºF/185ºC to allow the grill to preheat. Discard the marinade. Place the chicken in the grill and set the Timer to 5 minutes. When the Timer beeps, check the chicken with the tip of a knife. If the chicken is not cooked completely through, continue grilling for 1 to 2 minutes. **SERVES 4.**

NUTRITIONAL ANALYSIS: Calories: **205**   Total fat: **6g**   Saturated fat: **1g**   % calories from fat: **26**   Carbohydrates: **7 g**   Protein: **30 g**   Cholesterol: **74 mg**   Sodium: **385 mg**

LOW CARB

Pineapple Honey Chicken Breasts

The fresh flavor of pineapple combines with honey to produce a superior sauce.

1/4 c./60 ml.	**low sodium soy sauce**
1 t./5 g.	**ground ginger**
1 t./5 ml.	**vegetable oil**
1	**clove garlic, minced**
2 T./30 ml.	**honey**
4	**boneless, skinless chicken breast halves**
4	**fresh pineapple slices, 1/2-inch**/12 mm **thick**
	(4 canned pineapple slices may be substituted)

Blend together the soy sauce, ginger, oil, garlic and honey in a small bowl.

Set the Temperature to 375ºF/185ºC to allow the grill to preheat. Place the chicken in the grill and spoon the soy honey sauce over each piece. Close the grill and set the Timer for 3 minutes. The sauce will melt and run into the drip tray. When the Timer beeps, place 1 slice of pineapple on each piece of chicken and continue grilling for 2–4 minutes. If desired, you may pour the melted sauce over the grilled chicken to serve.

SERVES 4.

NUTRITIONAL ANALYSIS: Calories: **239** Total fat: **7g** Saturated fat: **1g**
% calories from fat: **26** Carbohydrates: **15 g** Protein: **29 g** Cholesterol: **73 mg** Sodium: **594 mg**

Chicken Yakitori Kebabs

Delectable kebabs for the entire family.

4	**boneless, skinless chicken breast halves**
2 t./10 ml.	**sesame oil**
2	**green/spring onions, finely chopped**
1/4 c./60 ml.	**low sodium soy sauce**
2 T./28 g.	**brown sugar**
2	**cloves garlic, finely minced**
8	**cherry tomatoes**
2	**small zucchini/courgettes, cut into 1/2-inch**/12 mm **pieces**
8	**10-inch**/25 cm **wooden skewers, soaked in water and drained**

Cut the chicken into 1-inch/2.5 cm cubes and place in a self-sealing plastic bag. Add the oil, onions, soy sauce, sugar and garlic. Refrigerate for 1 hour. To assemble the kebabs, thread the chicken, tomatoes and zucchini/courgettes onto the skewers alternately.

Set the Temperature to 350ºF /170ºC to allow the grill to preheat. Place the kebabs in the grill widthwise (horizontally) and close the grill. Set the Timer for 7 minutes. When the Timer beeps, check the chicken and if it is not completely cooked through, continue grilling for 1 to 2 minutes. **SERVES 4.**

NUTRITIONAL ANALYSIS: Calories: **236**   Total fat: **8g**   Saturated fat: **1g**   % calories from fat: **32**   Carbohydrates: **10 g**   Protein: **30 g**   Cholesterol: **73 mg**   Sodium: **599 mg**

LOW CARB

Turkey Pesto Pappardelle

*Pappardelle are fun, curly-edged noodles. If you can't find them,
you may substitute fettuccine or any other long pasta.*

10 oz./285 g.	**package frozen spinach, thawed**
1/2 c./115 g.	**fresh basil leaves, packed**
2 T./30 ml.	**extra virgin olive oil**
2 T./30 ml.	**lemon juice**
2	**cloves garlic, finely minced**
2 lbs./900 g.	**boneless, skinless turkey breast**
12 oz./340 g.	**pappardelle noodles, cooked**
4 oz./115 g.	**Parmesan cheese, grated**
4 oz./115 g.	**pine nuts**

Press as much liquid as possible from the spinach. Assemble the spinach, basil, oil, lemon juice and garlic and chop in a food processor until the mixture is well blended and smooth to create the pesto sauce. Cut the turkey into slices approximately one-half inch/2.5 cm. thick.

Set the Temperature to 350ºF /170ºC to allow the grill to preheat. Place the turkey slices in the grill and set the Timer to 5 minutes. When the Timer beeps, the turkey should be completely cooked through. If not, continue grilling for 1 to 2 minutes.

Toss the pesto with the noodles and divide evenly among 6 dinner plates. Add the grilled turkey slices on top and sprinkle with the Parmesan cheese and pine nuts. **SERVES 6.**

NUTRITIONAL ANALYSIS: Calories: **567**   Total fat: **27g**   Saturated fat: **8g**
% calories from fat: **44**   Carbohydrates: **24 g**   Protein: **51 g**   Cholesterol: **123 mg**   Sodium: **477 mg**

Yucatan Chicken Salsa

Accent this colorful meal with a fresh green salad.

4	boneless, skinless chicken breast halves
1/2 c./120 ml.	lime juice
1 t./5 g.	black pepper
1 t./5 g.	chili powder
1 T./15 ml.	extra virgin olive oil
1 c./225 g.	frozen corn kernels/sweetcorn, thawed
1	ripe tomato, seeded and chopped
1/4 c./55 g.	purple/red onion, chopped
1 T./15 ml.	lime juice
1/2 t./2.5 g.	ground cumin
4 c./900 g.	baked lowfat tortilla chips

Cut the chicken breasts into 1-inch/2.5 cm pieces and place in a medium bowl.
Combine the 1/2 cup/120 ml. lime juice, pepper, chili powder and oil and pour over
the chicken. Toss to blend. In a medium bowl, mix the corn, tomato, onion,
remaining lime juice and cumin to create the salsa. Set the Temperature to 350ºF
/170ºC to allow the grill to preheat. Place the chicken in the grill and set the Timer
to 7 minutes. When the Timer beeps, check the chicken with the tip of a knife. If
the chicken is not cooked completely through, continue grilling for 1 to 2 minutes.

Add the grilled chicken to the salsa and toss again. To serve, divide the
tortilla chips among 4 individual plates and top with the chicken salsa. **SERVES
4.**

NUTRITIONAL ANALYSIS: Calories: **206**   Total fat: **7g**   Saturated fat: **1g**
% calories from fat: **25**   Carbohydrates: **89 g**   Protein: **15 g**   Cholesterol: **73 mg**   Sodium: **413 mg**

Herbed Chicken & Mushroom Kebabs

Marinate the chicken and mushrooms at least 4 hours to absorb the mild herbs.

4	boneless, skinless chicken breast halves
1 lb./450 g.	fresh whole button mushrooms, cleaned and stems removed
1 t./5 g.	dried rosemary
1 T./14 g.	dried parsley
1/2 t./2.5 g.	dried thyme
1/4 c./60 ml.	lemon juice
2 T./30 ml.	white vinegar
1/2 c./120 ml.	nonfat chicken broth/stock
1 t./5 g.	black pepper
1/2 t./2.5 g.	salt
8	**10-inch**/25 cm **wooden skewers, soaked in water and drained**

Cut the chicken into 1-inch/2.5 cm pieces and place in a medium bowl. Add the mushrooms. Combine the rosemary, parsley, thyme, juice, vinegar, broth/stock, pepper and salt and pour over the chicken and mushrooms. Toss well. Marinate 4–12 hours in the refrigerator.

To assemble the kebabs, thread the chicken and mushrooms on the skewers and discard the marinade. Set the Temperature to 375ºF/185ºC to allow the grill to preheat. Place the chicken kebabs in the grill widthwise (horizontally) and set the Timer to 7 minutes. When the Timer beeps, check the chicken with the tip of a knife. If the chicken is not cooked completely through, continue grilling for 1 to 2 minutes. **SERVES 4.**

LOW CARB

NUTRITIONAL   ANALYSIS: Calories: **210**   Total fat: **6g**   Saturated fat: **1g**
% calories from fat: **26**   Carbohydrates: **8 g**   Protein: **31 g**   Cholesterol: **73 mg**   Sodium: **379 mg**

QUICK & EASY FAVORITES
—Burgers, Sandwiches & Snacks

Burgers, sandwiches and snacks have never been so easy to prepare and fun to eat as they are when grilled in *The George Foreman® Lean Mean Fat Reducing Grilling Machine!* As the recipes in this chapter demonstrate, you won't be bored with healthy burger choices such as *Hearty Tex-Mex Burgers, Stuffed Green Chile Burgers* and *Pineapple Teriyaki Burgers.* We've included recipes using ground beef, pork, chicken and turkey for variety and many types of sauces and ingredients to accompany them. Try them all—you'll soon find new favorites!

For an exciting change of pace, try grilling any of the sandwiches or snacks from our recipe collection. *Mediterranean Vegetable Sandwiches, Grilled Crab Lettuce Roll-Ups,* and *Poor Boy Steak Sandwiches* are just a few of the delicious, healthful sandwiches you can create. And, when you're ready to grill some very special snacks, we suggest our *Salami Supreme Calzone, Grilled Won Ton* or *Thai Beef Satay.*

Independence Day Burgers

*An all-time favorite made more healthful by using extra lean
ground round and whole grain hamburger buns.*

1 lb./450 g.	**extra lean ground round**
1 T./15 ml.	**Worcestershire sauce**
1 t./5 g.	**black pepper**
1 t./5 g.	**seasoned salt**
1	**purple/red onion, peeled**
4	**whole grain hamburger buns**

In a medium bowl, mix the beef, Worcestershire sauce, pepper and salt and shape into 4 hamburger patties. Slice the onion into 1/2-inch/12 mm thick slices without separating the rings.

Set the Temperature to 350ºF /170ºC to allow the grill to preheat. Place the hamburgers in the grill and set the Timer for 2 minutes. When the Timer beeps, add one full slice of onion to each burger and continue grilling for 2 to 3 minutes, or as desired. Serve the hamburgers on the buns and pass the condiments of your choice.

SERVES 4.

NUTRITIONAL ANALYSIS: Calories: **234**   Total fat: **11g**   Saturated fat: **4g**
% calories from fat: **47**   Carbohydrates: **40 g**   Protein: **24 g**   Cholesterol: **40 mg**   Sodium: **472 mg**

Cheesy Beef Burgers

Perfect for a break in the game.

1 lb./450 g.	lean ground chuck
1 c./225 g.	lowfat cheddar cheese, shredded
1 T./14 g.	green/spring onion, chopped
1 t./5 g.	salt
1/2 t./2.5 g.	black pepper
1/2 t./2.5 g.	garlic powder
1 T./15 ml.	Worcestershire sauce
4	sourdough hamburger buns, split

Mix together the beef, cheese, onion, salt, pepper, garlic powder and Worcestershire sauce and shape into 4 hamburger patties.

Set the Temperature to 350ºF /170ºC to allow the grill to preheat. Place the burgers in the grill and set the Timer to 4 minutes. When the Timer beeps, check the burgers and continue grilling if desired. To serve, place each burger on a sourdough bun and pass condiments of your choice.

SERVES 4.

NUTRITIONAL ANALYSIS: Calories: **484** Total fat: **16g** Saturated fat: **6g** % calories from fat: **30** Carbohydrates: **30 g** Protein: **52 g** Cholesterol: **121 mg** Sodium: **1,190 mg**

Hearty Tex-Mex Burgers

These are for the biggest appetites in the house!

2 lbs./900 g.	extra lean ground round
1⁄4 c./60 ml.	prepared barbeque sauce
1⁄4 c./55 g.	yellow/strong onion, finely chopped
2 T./30 ml.	fresh (or bottled) salsa
1 t./5 g.	chili powder
4	extra large hamburger buns

In a large bowl, thoroughly mix the beef, barbeque sauce, onion, salsa and chili powder. Shape into 4 large 3⁄4-inch/18 mm thick patties—these will be large!

Set the Temperature to 350ºF /170ºC to allow the grill to preheat. Place the burgers in the grill and set the Timer to 5 minutes. When the Timer beeps, check the burgers and continue grilling if desired. Serve the hamburgers on the buns and pass condiments of your choice.

SERVES 4.

NUTRITIONAL ANALYSIS: Calories: **714**   Total fat: **26g**   Saturated fat: **9g**
% calories from fat: **38**   Carbohydrates: **48 g**   Protein: **50 g**   Cholesterol: **83 mg**   Sodium: **441 mg**

Italiano Beef & Mozzarella Burgers

Serve open-faced on hearty peasant bread.

1 lb./450 g.	lean ground chuck
1 t./5 g.	ground oregano
1 t./5 g.	dried Italian seasoning
1	egg white
1	clove garlic, finely minced
2 T./28 g.	lowfat margarine
4	slices peasant bread/ciabatta, 1/2-inch/12 mm thick, lightly toasted
4	lettuce leaves
1	ripe tomato, thinly sliced
4	slices part-skim Mozzarella cheese
1/2	purple/red onion, thinly sliced
1⁄4 c./60 ml.	lowfat Italian salad dressing

Mix together the beef, oregano, Italian seasoning, egg white and garlic. Shape into 4 patties.

Set the Temperature to 350ºF /170ºC to allow the grill to preheat. Place the burgers in the grill and set the Timer to 4 minutes. When the Timer beeps, check the burgers and continue grilling if desired.

Spread the margarine on the bread and top each with the lettuce, tomato, cheese and onion. Drizzle the Italian salad dressing over all. Place the cooked hamburger patties on top and serve. **SERVES 4.**

NUTRITIONAL ANALYSIS: Calories: **424** Total fat: **15g** Saturated fat: **6g** % calories from fat: **33** Carbohydrates: **19 g** Protein: **49 g** Cholesterol: **132 mg** Sodium: **432 mg**

Barbequed Cowboy Burgers

Pack the burgers with crisp lettuce, tomatoes and dill pickles as condiments.

1/2 c./120 ml.	**tomato sauce**
3 T./42 g.	**yellow/strong onion, chopped**
1	**clove garlic, finely minced**
1 T./15 ml.	**prepared yellow mustard**
2 T./30 ml.	**Worcestershire sauce**
1 T./14 g.	**brown sugar**
1 lb./450 g.	**extra lean ground round**
4	**whole grain hamburger buns**

In a small saucepan, simmer together the tomato sauce, onion, garlic, mustard, Worcestershire sauce and brown sugar. Simmer for 10 minutes and cool completely. Mix the beef with the barbeque sauce in a large bowl. Shape into 4 patties and refrigerate at least 1 hour.

Set the Temperature to 350ºF /170ºC to allow the grill to preheat. Place the burgers in the grill and set the Timer to 4 minutes. When the Timer beeps, check the burgers and continue grilling if desired. Serve on the hamburger buns with condiments of your choice.

SERVES 4.

NUTRITIONAL ANALYSIS: Calories: **507**   Total fat: **21g**   Saturated fat: **5g**   % calories from fat: **38**   Carbohydrates: **49 g**   Protein: **27 g**   Cholesterol: **41 mg**   Sodium: **411 mg**

Sautéed Mushroom Burgers

Good enough for guests!

1/2 lb./225 g.	**fresh button mushrooms, cleaned and stems removed**
1 t./5 g.	**black pepper**
1 t./5 g.	**seasoned salt**
1/2 c./120 ml.	**nonfat beef broth/stock**
2 T./28 g.	**lowfat margarine**
1 lb./450 g.	**lean ground chuck**
8	**slices sweet French bread, 1/2-inch**/12 mm **thick, toasted**

Thinly slice the mushrooms into a sauté pan. Add the pepper, salt, broth/stock and margarine and heat. Simmer until the mushrooms are tender and the sauce is slightly condensed. Shape the beef into 4 patties.

Set the Temperature to 350ºF /170ºC to allow the grill to preheat. Place the burgers in the grill and set the Timer to 4 minutes. When the Timer beeps, check the burgers and continue grilling if desired.

Place 2 slices of bread on each plate and put a hamburger patty on one piece of the bread. Divide the sautéed mushrooms evenly over each hamburger and spoon additional sauce over each. Top with the second piece of bread.

SERVES 4.

NUTRITIONAL ANALYSIS: Calories: **393** Total fat: **10g** Saturated fat: **3g**
% calories from fat: **23** Carbohydrates: **29 g** Protein: **43 g** Cholesterol: **115 mg** Sodium: **865 mg**

Cheddar & Horseradish Beef Burgers

Zesty meets cheesy—and it's a good merger.

1 lb./450 g.	extra lean ground round
1/2 c./115 g.	lowfat cheddar cheese, grated
2 T./28 g.	cream-style horseradish
1/2 t./2.5 g.	black pepper
1/2 t./2.5 g.	salt
1/2 t./2.5 g.	garlic powder
4	onion rolls, toasted and split

In a medium bowl, combine the beef, cheese, horseradish, pepper, salt and garlic powder. Shape into 4 patties.

Set the Temperature to 350ºF /170ºC to allow the grill to preheat. Place the burgers in the grill and set the Timer to 4 minutes. When the Timer beeps, check the burgers and continue grilling if desired. Place the burgers on the onion rolls and accompany with the condiments of your choice.

SERVES 4.

NUTRITIONAL ANALYSIS: Calories: **428**   Total fat: **14g**   Saturated fat: **5g**
% calories from fat: **30**   Carbohydrates: **27 g**   Protein: **46 g**   Cholesterol: **118 mg**   Sodium: **747 mg**

Stuffed Green Chile Burgers

A favorite from sunny Arizona.

1 lb./450 g.	lean ground chuck
4	whole mild green chiles, canned
1/4 c./60 ml.	prepared salsa (fresh or canned)
1 t./5 g.	black pepper
4	slices lowfat Pepper Jack cheese/soft melting cheese with chili added to your taste
4	flour tortillas, warmed

Divide the beef into 4 portions. Divide each portion in half again and shape into thin patties. On top of 4 patties, place 1 green chile and 1 tablespoon/15 ml. of salsa. Sprinkle with black pepper and top with another beef patty, sealing the edges completely.

Set the Temperature to 350ºF /170ºC to allow the grill to preheat. Place the burgers in the grill and set the Timer to 4 minutes. When the Timer beeps, check the burgers and continue grilling if desired. Place each patty on 1 tortilla, top with 1 slice of the cheese and add condiments of your choice. Wrap the tortilla around the burger to serve.

SERVES 4.

NUTRITIONAL ANALYSIS: Calories: **459**   Total fat: **16g**   Saturated fat: **7g**
% calories from fat: **32**   Carbohydrates: **27 g**   Protein: **50 g**   Cholesterol: **135 mg**   Sodium: **641 mg**

Ranchero Burgers

Made with beef, beans and spices, these are surprisingly good—and good for you.

3/4 lb./340 g.	**extra lean ground round**
1/2 c./115 g.	**canned kidney beans, drained and mashed**
2	**cloves garlic, minced**
1/4 c./60 ml.	**prepared barbeque sauce**
1/2 t./2.5 g.	**salt**
1/2 t./2.5 g.	**black pepper**
4	**sesame-seeded hamburger buns**

Mix together thoroughly the beef, beans, garlic, barbeque sauce, salt and pepper. Shape into 4 patties.

Set the Temperature to 350ºF /170ºC to allow the grill to preheat. Place the burgers in the grill and set the Timer to 4 minutes. When the Timer beeps, check the burgers and continue grilling if desired. Place each hamburger on a sesame bun and serve with your choice of condiments.

SERVES 4.

NUTRITIONAL ANALYSIS: Calories: **502**   Total fat: **19g**   Saturated fat: **4g**   % calories from fat: **35**   Carbohydrates: **57 g**   Protein: **23 g**   Cholesterol: **31 mg**   Sodium: **663 mg**

Asian Chicken Burgers

Soy sauce, garlic and onions make these burgers unique.

1 lb./450 g.	lean ground chicken
1 T./15 ml.	lemon juice
1	clove garlic, minced
2	green/spring onions, finely chopped
2 T./30 ml.	low sodium soy sauce
1/2 t./2.5 g.	ground ginger
1	egg white
4	sesame seeded hamburger buns

In a large bowl, combine the chicken, lemon juice, garlic, onions, soy sauce, ginger and egg white. Shape into 4 patties. Refrigerate for 1 hour.

Set the Temperature to 350ºF /170ºC and allow the grill to preheat. Place the burgers in the grill and set the Timer to 5 minutes. When the Timer beeps, check the burgers and continue grilling until the chicken is completely cooked through. Serve on the sesame seeded buns and pass condiments such as lowfat peanut butter, hoisin sauce and bean sprouts.

SERVES 4.

NUTRITIONAL ANALYSIS: Calories: **721** Total fat: **16g** Saturated fat: **>1g** % calories from fat: **19** Carbohydrates: **38 g** Protein: **16 g** Cholesterol: **0 mg** Sodium: **823 mg**

Ranch Style Chicken Burgers

These burgers are full of surprising ingredients.

1 lb./450 g.	lean ground chicken
1/4 t./1 g.	garlic powder
1/2 t./2.5 ml.	Tabasco sauce
1/4 t./1 g.	seasoned salt
1/2 t./2.5 g.	black pepper, coarsely ground
1 T./14 g.	fresh cilantro/coriander leaves, finely minced
2 T./28 g.	diced green chile peppers, canned
2 T./30 ml.	nonfat ranch salad dressing
4	hamburger buns

Mix together the chicken, garlic powder, Tabasco sauce, salt, pepper, cilantro/coriander leaves, chile peppers and salad dressing. Shape into 4 patties.

Set the Temperature to 350°F /170°C to allow the grill to preheat. Place the burgers in the grill and set the Timer to 5 minutes. When the Timer beeps, check the burgers and continue grilling until the chicken is completely cooked through. Place each patty on a bun and serve with condiments of your choice.

SERVES 4.

NUTRITIONAL ANALYSIS: Calories: **567** Total fat: **17g** Saturated fat: **>1g**
% calories from fat: **19** Carbohydrates: **93 g** Protein: **17 g** Cholesterol: **0 mg** Sodium: **1,213 mg**

Pineapple Teriyaki Burgers

Simple ingredients and delicious taste.

1 lb./450 g.	**lean ground chicken**
1	**egg white**
1/4 c./60 ml.	**bottled teriyaki sauce**
1/4 c./55 g.	**yellow/strong onion, chopped**
1/2 t./2.5 g.	**black pepper**
1 t./5 ml.	**prepared mustard**
4	**slices fresh pineapple, 1/4-inch**/6 mm **thick**
	(or 4 canned slices, if desired)
4	**sesame seed hamburger buns**

Combine the chicken, egg white, teriyaki sauce, onion, pepper and mustard in a medium bowl. Shape into 4 patties.

Set the Temperature to 350ºF /170ºC and allow the grill to preheat. Place the burgers on the grill and set the Timer to 3 minutes. When the Timer beeps, open the grill and add 1 slice of pineapple to each patty. Grill for 2 minutes, or until the chicken is completely cooked through. Serve on sesame seed hamburger buns or over steamed brown rice.

SERVES 4.

NUTRITIONAL ANALYSIS: Calories: **749**   Total fat: **16g**   Saturated fat: **>1g**
% calories from fat: **18**   Carbohydrates: **144 g**   Protein: **17 g**   Cholesterol: **0 mg**   Sodium: **1,263 mg**

Down Home Turkey Burgers

Savor the hickory-smoked flavor.

1 lb./450 g.	lean ground turkey
2 T./30 ml.	liquid smoke/barbecue flavoring
1	egg white
1	clove garlic, minced
2 T./30 ml.	hickory-flavored barbeque sauce
2 T./28 g.	white onion, finely chopped
1/4 c./55 g.	fresh bread crumbs
1 t./5 g.	salt
1/2 t./2.5 g.	black pepper
4	whole grain hamburger buns

Mix together the turkey, liquid smoke/barbecue flavoring, egg white, garlic, barbeque sauce, onion, bread crumbs, salt and pepper. Shape into 4 patties.

Set the Temperature to 350ºF /170ºC to allow the grill to preheat. Place the burgers in the grill and set the Timer to 7 minutes. When the Timer beeps, check the burgers and continue grilling until the turkey is completely cooked through. Place each patty on a hamburger bun and pass with your choice of accompaniments.

SERVES 4.

NUTRITIONAL ANALYSIS: Calories: **448**   Total fat: **20g**   Saturated fat: **3g**
% calories from fat: **36**   Carbohydrates: **50 g**   Protein: **27 g**   Cholesterol: **64 mg**   Sodium: **837 mg**

Swiss Turkey Burgers

The cheese adds a delectable flavor!

1 lb./450 g.	**lean ground turkey**
6 oz./170 g.	**lowfat Swiss cheese, shredded**
1	**egg white**
1 T./15 ml.	**Dijon mustard**
1/4 c./55 g.	**fresh bread crumbs**
1 t./5 g.	**black pepper**
1 t./5 g.	**seasoned salt**
4	**onion rolls, split**

Combine the turkey, Swiss cheese, egg white, mustard, bread crumbs, pepper and salt in a medium bowl. Shape into 4 patties.

Set the Temperature to 350ºF /170ºC to allow the grill to preheat. Place the burgers in the grill and set the Timer to 7 minutes. When the Timer beeps, check the burgers and continue grilling until the turkey is completely cooked through. Place each burger in a roll and serve with condiments of your choice.

SERVES 4.

NUTRITIONAL ANALYSIS: Calories: **409**   Total fat: **13g**   Saturated fat: **5g**
% calories from fat: **27**   Carbohydrates: **34 g**   Protein: **41 g**   Cholesterol: **79 mg**   Sodium: **958 mg**

Turkey Burgers with Cranberry Glaze

Enjoy the essence of turkey and cranberry!

1 lb./450 g.	lean ground turkey
1	egg white
1 T./15 ml.	Worcestershire sauce
1	clove garlic, minced
1 t./5 g.	black pepper
1/2 c./115 g.	jellied cranberry sauce, canned
1 t./5 ml.	lemon juice
4	whole wheat hamburger buns, split
4	romaine lettuce leaves
1/4 c./55 g.	walnuts, finely chopped

Combine the turkey, egg white, Worcestershire sauce, garlic and pepper and shape into 4 burgers. Combine the cranberry sauce and lemon juice in a small saucepan and heat until it is smooth. Set the Temperature to 350ºF /170ºC to allow the grill to preheat. Place the turkey patties in the grill and smooth 1 tablespoon/15 ml. of the glaze over each. Set the Timer to 4 minutes. When the Timer beeps, check the burgers and add sauce again. Set the Timer to 3 minutes. When the Timer beeps, check the turkey and continue grilling until completely cooked through.

To serve, place the buns on individual plates. Put one lettuce leaf on one half of the bun, place the turkey burger over that, spoon additional sauce over the patty and sprinkle chopped walnuts over all.

SERVES 4.

NUTRITIONAL   ANALYSIS: Calories: **513**   Total fat: **24g**   Saturated fat: **3g**
% calories from fat: **38**   Carbohydrates: **57 g**   Protein: **28 g**   Cholesterol: **64 mg**   Sodium: **173 mg**

Dijon Pork Burgers

*Ground pork is very lean, but can be made tender and moist with
the addition of mayonnaise and Dijon mustard.*

1 lb./450 g.	**lean ground pork**
2 T./30 ml.	**Dijon mustard**
2 T./30 ml.	**nonfat mayonnaise**
2 T./28 g.	**white onion, chopped**
1 t./5 g.	**black pepper**
1/2 t./2.5 g.	**salt**
4	**Kaiser rolls/crusty dinner rolls, split**

Combine the pork, mustard, mayonnaise, onion, pepper and salt. Shape into 4 burgers.

Set the Temperature to 350ºF /170ºC to allow the grill to preheat. Place the burgers in the grill and set the Timer to 7 minutes. When the Timer beeps, check the burgers and continue grilling if desired. Serve on Kaiser rolls/crusty dinner rolls with condiments of your choice.

SERVES 4.

NUTRITIONAL ANALYSIS: Calories: **364** Total fat: **15g** Saturated fat: **3g**
% calories from fat: **37** Carbohydrates: **30 g** Protein: **26 g** Cholesterol: **32 mg** Sodium: **869 mg**

Mediterranean Lamb Burgers

An intriguing twist on conventional beef hamburgers.

1 lb./450 g.	lean ground lamb
1/2 t./2.5 g.	black pepper, coarsely ground
1/2 t./2.5 g.	dried rosemary
1/2 t./2.5 g.	salt
2 T./28 g.	purple/red onion, chopped
1 T./15 ml.	lemon juice
1 T./15 ml.	prepared yellow mustard
4	soft pita breads (or hamburger buns, if desired)
	sliced purple/red onions
	romaine lettuce leaves
	sliced cucumber
	sliced tomatoes

Combine the lamb, pepper, rosemary, salt, onion, juice and mustard in a medium bowl. Shape into 4 patties.

Set the Temperature to 350ºF /170ºC to allow the grill to preheat. Place the burgers in the grill and set the Timer to 6 minutes. When the Timer beeps, check the burgers and continue grilling if desired.

Serve in the pita pockets and pass the onions, lettuce, cucumber and tomatoes as condiments. **SERVES 4.**

NUTRITIONAL ANALYSIS: Calories: **443**   Total fat: **20g**   Saturated fat: **7g**
% calories from fat: **40**   Carbohydrates: **42 g**   Protein: **27 g**   Cholesterol: **75 mg**   Sodium: **747 mg**

Santa Fe Veggie Burgers

Meatless burgers made great with veggies and spices.

1 c./225 g.	steamed white rice, cooked and cooled
1/2 c./115 g.	corn kernels/sweetcorn, canned
1	green pepper, seeded and finely chopped
1/2 c./115 g.	white onion, finely chopped
1 t./5 g.	black pepper, coarsely ground
1 t./5 g.	salt
1 t./5 ml.	lemon juice
1 t./5 g.	chili powder
4	whole grain hamburger buns

In the bowl of a food processor, combine the rice, corn, green pepper, onion, pepper, salt, juice and chili powder. Pulse rapidly to produce a coarse, mealy texture. Shape the vegetable-rice mixture into 4 patties and refrigerate for 2 hours.

Set the Temperature to 350ºF /170ºC to allow the grill to preheat. Place the patties in the grill and set the Timer for 4 minutes. Remove the burgers and place the patties in the hamburger buns. Top with your choice of accompaniments.

SERVES 4.

NUTRITIONAL ANALYSIS: Calories: **357**   Total fat: **13g**   Saturated fat: **>1g**
% calories from fat: **32**   Carbohydrates: **58 g**   Protein: **5 g**   Cholesterol: **0 mg**   Sodium: **64 mg**

Portabella Mushroom Burgers

A meatless burger with a fresh, savory flavor.

4	**Portabella mushrooms, cleaned and stems removed**
2 T./30 ml.	**extra virgin olive oil**
2 T./30 ml.	**balsamic vinegar**
2	**cloves garlic, finely minced**
1 T./14 g.	**dried Italian seasoning**
1 t./5 g.	**black pepper, coarsely ground**
4	**Kaiser rolls/crusty dinner rolls, split**

Set the Temperature to 350ºF /170ºC to allow the grill to preheat.Place the mushrooms in the grill, underside facing up. Drizzle the oil and vinegar over each mushroom and sprinkle with the garlic, Italian seasoning and pepper. Close the grill and set the Timer to 5 minutes. The mushrooms should be tender when done.

Serve in Kaiser rolls/crusty dinner rolls and pass condiments such as sliced onion, lowfat Mozzarella cheese, tomato, etc.

SERVES 4.

NUTRITIONAL ANALYSIS: Calories: **256**   Total fat: **13g**   Saturated fat: **3g**
% calories from fat: **44**   Carbohydrates: **31 g**   Protein: **6 g**   Cholesterol: **0 mg**   Sodium: **312 mg**

SANDWICHES & SNACKS
Hot Sausage Sandwiches

Look for Italian sausage links in the fresh meat section of your grocery store.

1 lb./450 g.	lowfat hot Italian sausage links/bangers
1	ripe tomato, sliced
1	green pepper, seeded and thinly sliced
1	small purple/red onion, thinly sliced
1	clove garlic, finely minced
1 t./5 g.	black pepper, coarsely ground
1 t./5 g.	dried Italian seasoning
1/4 c./60 ml.	nonfat mayonnaise
4	hero sandwich buns/soft buns, split and toasted

Set the Temperature to 350ºF /170ºC to allow the grill to preheat. Arrange the sausages/bangers widthwise (horizontally) on the grill and place the tomato, green pepper and onion around the links. Mix together the garlic, black pepper and Italian seasoning and sprinkle over the sausage-vegetable mixture.

Close the grill and set the Timer for 6 minutes. When the Timer beeps, the vegetables should be tender and the sausage/bangers heated through. If not, continue grilling for 1 to 2 minutes. Lightly spread the mayonnaise on each split bun and mound the sausage vegetable mixture inside.

SERVES 4.

NUTRITIONAL ANALYSIS: Calories: **469**   Total fat: **17g**   Saturated fat: **5g**
% calories from fat: **31**   Carbohydrates: **49 g**   Protein: **31 g**   Cholesterol: **80 mg**   Sodium: **798 mg**

Salami Supreme Calzone

Grilled Calzone? You won't believe it until you try these delicious sandwich pockets!

1 loaf	frozen bread dough, thawed
6 T./90 ml.	tomato sauce
1	clove garlic, finely minced
1 T./14 g.	fresh parsley, finely minced
1 t./5 g.	dried Italian seasoning
1/2 t./2.5 g.	ground oregano
1 t./5 g.	black pepper
16	slices lowfat salami
1/2 c./115 g.	yellow/strong onion, finely chopped
1 c./225 g.	lowfat Mozzarella cheese, shredded

Divide the dough into 4 equal pieces. Reserve 2 pieces for another use. On a lightly floured board, roll out each of the remaining 2 pieces into a circle about 8 inches/20 cm in diameter and 1/8-inch/3 mm thick.

Spoon the tomato sauce over one half of each dough circle. Add the garlic, parsley, Italian seasoning, oregano and black pepper. Top each half with salami, onion and cheese. Fold each remaining half circle of dough over the toppings and press the edges together to form a tight seal.

Set the Temperature to 350ºF /170ºC and allow the grill to preheat. Place one calzone in the grill and set the Timer for 4 minutes. When the Timer beeps, check the calzone and continue grilling if needed. Repeat with the remaining calzone.

MAKES 2 CALZONE, ENOUGH FOR 4 SERVINGS.

NUTRITIONAL ANALYSIS: Calories: **621**   Total fat: **24g**   Saturated fat: **10g**   % calories from fat: **36**   Carbohydrates: **67 g**   Protein: **29 g**   Cholesterol: **36 mg**   Sodium: **2,398 mg**

Poor Boy Steak Sandwiches

Originally conceived as a "poor man's meal," using bits of leftover meat, today's poor boy sandwiches are packed with juicy chuck steak and savory flavors.

1 lb./450 g.	beef chuck steak
1 t./5 g.	black pepper
1/2 t./2.5 g.	salt
1	**4 oz.**/115 g. **can diced green chiles**
1	small tomato, diced
1 T./15 ml.	Dijon mustard
1 T./15 ml.	extra virgin olive oil
4	large hero-style sandwich buns/soft buns, split and toasted

Remove any visible fat from the steak and slice the steak in thin strips across the grain of the meat. Set the Temperature to 400ºF/200ºC to allow the grill to preheat. Place the steak in the grill and sprinkle with pepper and salt. Set the Timer for 2 minutes. When the Timer beeps, add the green chiles and tomato. Set the Timer for 2 minutes. When the Timer beeps, remove the steak from the grill and set aside.

Spread the Dijon mustard on one side of each bun and drizzle the olive oil on the other. Pack the meat mixture inside each hero and serve with onions, if desired.

SERVES 4.

NUTRITIONAL ANALYSIS: Calories: **445**   Total fat: **12g**   Saturated fat: **5g**   % calories from fat: **25**   Carbohydrates: **36 g**   Protein: **45 g**   Cholesterol: **114 mg**   Sodium: **945 mg**

Grilled Garden Vegetable Sandwiches

A healthy alternative to fast-food lunches.

2	zucchini/courgettes, thinly sliced
1/2	small purple/red onion, thinly sliced
1	red pepper, seeded and thinly sliced
10	shiitake mushrooms, thinly sliced
1 c./225 g.	eggplant/aubergine, diced
1 T./15 ml.	extra virgin olive oil
1	clove garlic, finely minced
1 t./5 g.	black pepper, coarsely ground
1/2 t./2.5 g.	salt
4	onion rolls, split and toasted
1/4 c./55 g.	lowfat Parmesan cheese, grated

Set the Temperature to 350ºF /170ºC to allow the grill to preheat. Carefully open the grill and layer the zucchini/courgettes, onion, red pepper, mushrooms and eggplant/aubergine on the grilling plate. Sprinkle the oil, garlic, pepper and salt over the vegetables.

Close the grill and set the Timer for 5 minutes. Top each roll with equal portions of the vegetables and sprinkle Parmesan cheese over each sandwich.

SERVES 4.

NUTRITIONAL ANALYSIS: Calories: **262**   Total fat: **10g**   Saturated fat: **2g**
% calories from fat: **32**   Carbohydrates: **35 g**   Protein: **11 g**   Cholesterol: **5 mg**   Sodium: **680 mg**

Grilled Crab Lettuce Roll-ups

Delicate wraps are perfect for a light luncheon.

12 oz./340 g.	**fresh crabmeat, or 12 oz.**/340 g. **canned crabmeat, drained**
1 c./225 g.	**fresh bread crumbs (white or whole wheat)**
1/2 c./115 g.	**white onion, finely chopped**
1/2 c./120 ml.	**nonfat mayonnaise**
1 T./15 ml.	**Dijon mustard**
1/2 t./2.5 g.	**black pepper**
1/2 t./2.5 g.	**salt**
8	**large romaine or butter lettuce leaves, cleaned and drained**
1/4 c./60 ml.	**prepared crab cocktail sauce**

Set the Temperature to 300ºF/140ºC to allow the grill to preheat. Combine the crabmeat, bread crumbs, onion, mayonnaise, mustard, pepper and salt. Lightly spread the mixture in the grill, using the plastic spatula.

Set the Timer to 3 minutes. When the Timer beeps, the crab mixture should be heated through and lightly browned. If not, continue grilling for 1 to 2 minutes. Using the plastic spatula, remove the crab filling from the grill and place on 4 individual plates.

To assemble, place a heaping spoonful of crab on each lettuce leaf and roll up. Dip the lettuce into the cocktail sauce, as desired.

MAKES 8 ROLL-UPS, ENOUGH FOR 4 SERVINGS.

NUTRITIONAL ANALYSIS: Calories: **269**   Total fat: **3g**   Saturated fat: **>1g**
% calories from fat: **11**   Carbohydrates: **32 g**   Protein: **23 g**   Cholesterol: **60 mg**   Sodium: **1,228 mg**

Grilled Ahi Tuna Sandwiches

Select very fresh Ahi tuna and grill the tuna to rare or medium-rare for best results.

1 t./5 g.	ground ginger
1 T./15 ml.	low sodium soy sauce
1 t./5 g.	garlic powder
1 T./15 ml.	lemon juice
4	4 oz./115 g. **Ahi tuna steaks**
1/4 c./60 ml.	nonfat mayonnaise
4	4-inch/10 cm **French bread rolls**
	fresh butter lettuce leaves
1	small ripe tomato, thinly sliced

In a small bowl, combine the ginger, soy sauce, garlic powder and lemon juice. Set the Temperature to 375ºF/ 185ºC to allow the grill to preheat. Place the tuna in the grill and spoon the ginger soy sauce over each piece. Set the Timer to 4 minutes. When the Timer beeps, check the tuna and continue grilling 1 to 2 minutes if preferred.

Lightly spread the mayonnaise on the French bread rolls, layer with the lettuce and tomato and place the grilled tuna on top.

SERVES 4.

NUTRITIONAL ANALYSIS: Calories: **294** Total fat: **6g** Saturated fat: **>1g** % calories from fat: **18** Carbohydrates: **25 g** Protein: **39 g** Cholesterol: **66 mg** Sodium: **704 mg**

Chicken Cheese Quesadillas

A simple "quick-fix" for any time of the day.

2	**boneless, skinless chicken breast halves**
4	**flour tortillas**
1 c./225 g.	**lowfat cheddar cheese**
2 T./28 g.	**green/spring onion, chopped**
1/2 c./120 ml.	**prepared mild tomato salsa**

Set the Temperature to 375ºF/185ºC and allow the grill to preheat. Place the chicken in the grill and set the Timer to 5 minutes. When the Timer beeps, check the chicken with the tip of a knife. If the chicken is not cooked completely through, continue grilling for 1 to 2 minutes. Cool and chop into small pieces.

On one half of one tortilla, place one-fourth of the chicken, cheese, onion and salsa. Fold the top half over the cheese and chicken. Set the Temperature to 400ºF/200ºC and place the quesadilla in the grill. Set the Timer for 3 minutes and grill until the quesadilla is lightly browned and the cheese is melted. Remove and grill the remaining quesadillas as directed above.

SERVES 4.

NUTRITIONAL ANALYSIS: Calories: **342**   Total fat: **11g**   Saturated fat: **3g**   % calories from fat: **28**   Carbohydrates: **42 g**   Protein: **18 g**   Cholesterol: **16 mg**   Sodium: **624 mg**

Thai Beef Satay

An excellent appetizer or snack.

1 1/2 lb./680 g.	**beef top round**
1/2 c./120 ml.	**low sodium soy sauce**
1/2 t./2.5 g.	**ground ginger**
1	**clove garlic, minced**
1 t./5 ml.	**white vinegar**
1	**green/spring onion, finely chopped**
1 T./14 g.	**honey**
10	**8-inch**/20 cm **wooden skewers, soaked in water and drained**
2 oz./55 g.	**dry-roasted peanuts, chopped**

Cut the beef into very thin slices and place in a large self-sealing plastic bag. In a small serving bowl, combine the soy sauce, ginger, garlic, vinegar, onion and honey and pour over the beef. Seal the bag, removing as much air as possible, and refrigerate for 6–10 hours.

Thread the beef slices through the skewers in an accordion fashion, adjusting the meat to uniformly fit the skewers. Discard the marinade. Set the Temperature to 400ºF/200ºC to allow the grill to preheat. Place the satay skewers in the grill widthwise (horizontally).

Close the grill and set the Timer for 3 minutes. When the Timer beeps, check the beef and continue grilling, if desired. Sprinkle each skewer with the chopped peanuts just before serving. **SERVES 10.**

NUTRITIONAL ANALYSIS: Calories: **153**   Total fat: **6g**   Saturated fat: **2g**
% calories from fat: **37**   Carbohydrates: **4 g**   Protein: **17 g**   Cholesterol: **41 mg**   Sodium: **462 mg**

Grilled Won Ton

Won ton aren't typically grilled, but The George Foreman® Lean Mean
Fat Reducing Grilling Machine makes this easy.

2	**boneless, skinless chicken breast halves**
1/4 c./55 g.	**water chestnuts, finely diced**
1/2 c./115 g.	**bean sprouts, finely chopped**
1	**clove garlic, finely minced**
2 T./30 ml.	**low sodium soy sauce**
1/4 c./60 ml.	**hoisin sauce**
1 T./15 ml.	**Szechuan chili sauce**
16	**won ton noodle squares**

Set the Temperature to 375ºF/185ºC to allow the grill to preheat. Place the chicken in the grill and set the Timer to 5 minutes. When the Timer beeps, check the chicken with the tip of a knife. If the chicken is not cooked completely through, continue grilling for 1 to 2 minutes. Cool and chop into very small pieces. Combine the chicken, water chestnuts, bean sprouts, garlic, soy sauce, hoisin sauce and chili sauce. Mix well. Place 1 won ton square on a flat surface. Spoon 1 heaping tablespoon/20 ml. of the chicken and vegetable mixture on one-half of the square.

Dab a bit of water on the edges of the noodle and fold the remaining half of the noodle over the top, forming a triangle and sealing the edges with your fingertips. Repeat with the remaining won ton noodle squares.

Set the Temperature to 375ºF/185ºC to allow the grill to preheat. Place 4 won ton in the grill and set the Timer for 5 minutes. Repeat with the remaining won ton. Serve with additional soy sauce, if desired. **SERVES 8.**

NUTRITIONAL ANALYSIS: Calories: **122** Total fat: **1g** Saturated fat: **>1g**
% calories from fat: **11** Carbohydrates: **15 g** Protein: **9 g** Cholesterol: **20 mg** Sodium: **382 mg**

TEMPTING COMPANION DISHES
—Vegetables, Fruit, Salads & Desserts

Your *George Foreman® Lean Mean Fat Reducing Grilling Machine* brings out the very best of vegetables and fruit. If you can imagine tender-crisp grilled vegetables and warm, sweet grilled fruit, you'll enjoy the wide variety of recipes that follow in this chapter. From *Creamy Dill Carrots* and *Cheesy Grilled New Potatoes* to *Quick & Easy Grilled Bananas* and *Grilled Apple Pecan Cups,* you'll find vegetable and fruit dishes to satisfy every appetite. Also, because fruit is so naturally sweet, we've included recipes for fruit desserts that are quick and easy to prepare.

Vegetables are typically lowfat and naturally healthful food choices. Grilling complements vegetables by releasing natural liquids and expanding the true flavor of the vegetables. Vegetables should be uniformly cut or sliced and they should be 1 inch/2.5 cm or less in thickness in order to properly grill. Firm vegetables work especially well in the grill, including squash/courgettes, eggplant/aubergine, potatoes, Brussels sprouts and carrots. Herbs and spices with lemon or vinegar add a dash of personality to the vegetables as they grill. If you prefer, you may also marinate vegetables and then grill them for added flavor.

Fruit is, without a doubt, the most wonderful and natural salad or dessert when it is grilled to tenderness. The quick, hot grilling process seals in the fruit juice and warms the fruit very rapidly. Firm fruits such as apples, pineapple, peaches, bananas and nectarines grill nicely. Because fruit will lose its texture and become mushy when overcooked, always watch the grill carefully and check the fruit a few minutes before it's supposed to be done. Perfectly grilled fruit is tender-crisp and warm throughout. For a dessert treat, combine grilled fruit with lowfat frozen yogurt or fat-free pudding.

Hearty salads begin with *The George Foreman® Lean Mean Fat Reducing Grilling Machine*. Whether you choose to grill a small sirloin steak for a large Asian noodle salad, or build a chicken Caesar salad by grilling tender chicken breast strips, you'll find that the grill is the start of unique and delicious salads.

VEGETABLES
Italian Portabella Mushrooms

Lightly grill tender mushrooms for a fresh-roasted flavor.

4	mushrooms, cleaned, dried and stems removed
1 T./15 ml.	extra virgin olive oil
1 t./5 ml.	balsamic vinegar
1/4 t./1 g.	dried Italian seasoning
1/4 t./1 g.	black pepper
1/2 t./2.5 g.	salt

Arrange the mushrooms on a flat tray, with the undersides facing up. Mix together the oil, vinegar, Italian seasoning, pepper and salt and lightly drizzle over the mushrooms.

Set the Temperature to 350ºF/170ºC to allow the grill to preheat. Place the mushrooms in the grill, undersides facing up, and set the Timer 5 minutes. When the Timer beeps, remove the mushrooms and cool slightly.

To serve, cut each mushroom into 4 wedges and arrange on a serving platter.

SERVES 4.

NUTRITIONAL ANALYSIS: Calories: **226** Total fat: **6g** Saturated fat: **2g** % calories from fat: **28** Carbohydrates: **31 g** Protein: **6 g** Cholesterol: **0 mg** Sodium: **310 mg**

Rosemary Brussels Sprouts

The light herb and butter flavors accentuate the bold flavors of the sprouts.

16 oz./450 g.	package frozen Brussels sprouts, thawed and drained
1/2 t./2.5 g.	fresh rosemary, finely minced
2 T./28 g.	lowfat margarine
1/2 t./2.5 g.	garlic salt
1/4 t./1 g.	black pepper

Pat the sprouts dry and cut each in half. In a small bowl, mix together the rosemary, lowfat margarine, garlic salt and pepper.

Set the Temperature to 350ºF/170ºC to allow the grill to preheat. Place the sprouts in the grill and spread the herb butter over the sprouts. Set the Timer to 8 minutes. As the herb butter melts, it will drip into the grilling tray. To serve, spoon the sprouts into a bowl and pour the melted herb butter over them.

SERVES 4.

LOW CARB

NUTRITIONAL ANALYSIS: Calories: **87** Total fat: **4g** Saturated fat: **>1g**
% calories from fat: **39** Carbohydrates: **10 g** Protein: **4 g** Cholesterol: **0 mg** Sodium: **276 mg**

Grilled Winter Squash

This is super-quick and easy.

1 lb./450 g.	**winter squash**
2 T./28 g.	**lowfat margarine**
1/2 t./2.5 g.	**black pepper**
1/2 t./2.5 g.	**seasoned salt**

Clean the squash and remove the seeds and woody fibers. Dice the squash into small cubes about 1/4-inch/6-mm square. Mix together the lowfat margarine, black pepper and salt in a small bowl.

Set the Temperature to 325ºF/155ºC to allow the grill to preheat. Place the squash in the grill and brush with the butter mixture. Close the grill and set the Timer to 6 minutes. As the herb butter melts, it will drip into the grilling tray. To serve, place the squash in a serving bowl and pour the melted, seasoned butter over the squash.

SERVES 4.

NUTRITIONAL ANALYSIS: Calories: **50** Total fat: **1g** Saturated fat: **>1g** % calories from fat: **24** Carbohydrates: **9 g** Protein: **>1 g** Cholesterol: **0 mg** Sodium: **213 mg**

Grilled Garlic Zucchini/Courgettes

A hearty garlic spread accompanies the mild squash flavor.

3	zucchini/courgettes, medium-sized
2 T./30 ml.	extra virgin olive oil
2 T./30 ml.	lemon juice
2	cloves garlic, finely minced
1/4 t./1 g.	black pepper, coarsely ground
1/2 t./2.5 g.	salt

Peel the zucchini/courgettes and cut lengthwise into thin matchstick pieces. Combine the oil, lemon juice, garlic, pepper and salt in a medium-sized bowl. Toss the zucchini/courgettes with the garlic mixture and let stand for 10 minutes to allow the zucchini/courgettes to absorb the flavors.

Set the Temperature to 325ºF/155ºC to allow the grill to preheat. Place the zucchini/courgettes in the grill widthwise (horizontally) and set the Timer for 5 minutes. The zucchini/courgettes should be tender-crisp when done.

SERVES 4.

LOW CARB

NUTRITIONAL ANALYSIS: Calories: **40**   Total fat: **3g**   Saturated fat: **>1g**   % calories from fat: **50**   Carbohydrates: **4 g**   Protein: **2 g**   Cholesterol: **0 mg**   Sodium: **3 mg**

Creamy Dill Carrots

Grilled sweet carrots smothered with a tangy sauce—delicious!

10	**fresh carrots, peeled**
1/4 c./60 ml.	**lowfat mayonnaise**
1/4 c./60 ml.	**lowfat sour cream**
1 t./5 g.	**fresh dill, finely minced**
1/2 t./2.5 ml.	**lemon juice**
1/2 t./2.5 g.	**black pepper**
1 t./5 ml.	**nonfat milk**
1 T./15 ml.	**extra virgin olive oil**

Cut each carrot in half lengthwise and in half widthwise. Combine the mayonnaise, sour cream, dill, lemon juice, pepper and milk in a small bowl. Blend thoroughly, cover and store in the refrigerator until ready to use.

Set the Temperature to 350ºF/170ºC to allow the grill to preheat. Place the carrots widthwise (horizontally) in the grill, cut side up and lightly drizzle with the oil. Close the grill and set the Timer to 5 minutes. When the Timer beeps, check the carrots with a fork. They will be tender-crisp when done.

To serve, place the carrots in a warmed serving dish and pass the dill sauce as an accompaniment.

SERVES 4.

NUTRITIONAL ANALYSIS: Calories: **137** Total fat: **4g** Saturated fat: **>1g**
% calories from fat: **23** Carbohydrates: **25 g** Protein: **3 g** Cholesterol: **1 mg** Sodium: **181 mg**

Zesty Marinated Zucchini

A splash of balsamic vinegar and oil creates a Tuscan delight.

4	medium-sized zucchini/courgettes
3 T./45 ml.	extra virgin olive oil
1/4 c./60 ml.	lemon juice
1 T./15 ml.	balsamic vinegar
2	cloves garlic, finely minced
1/2 t./2.5 g.	dried basil
1 t./5 g.	black pepper
1/4 t./1 g.	salt

Scrub the zucchini/courgettes and cut into slices 1/2-inch/12-mm thick. In a 9-inch x 9-inch/23 cm x 23 cm glass pan, combine the oil, lemon juice, vinegar, garlic, basil, pepper and salt. Add the zucchini/courgettes and mix well. Cover with plastic wrap and refrigerate overnight.

Set the Temperature to 325ºF/155ºC to allow the grill to preheat. Place the zucchini/courgettes in the grill in overlapping slices and set the Timer to 6 minutes. When the Timer beeps, check the squash with the tip of a knife. It will be tender-crisp when done. Serve on a warmed platter.

SERVES 6.

LOW CARB

NUTRITIONAL ANALYSIS: Calories: **8**   Total fat: **>1g**   Saturated fat: **>1g**
% calories from fat: **49**   Carbohydrates: **>1 g**   Protein: **>1 g**   Cholesterol: **0 mg**   Sodium: **17 mg**

Italian Yellow Squash

Serve with lamb, chicken or turkey.

1 lb./450 g.	**yellow squash**
1 T./14 g.	**fresh parsley, finely minced**
1 t./5 g.	**dried Italian seasoning**
1/2 t./2.5 g.	**ground oregano**
2 T./30 ml.	**extra-virgin olive oil**
1 T./15 ml.	**balsamic vinegar**
1/2 t./2.5 g.	**black pepper**

Clean the squash and cut into slices 1/4-inch/6-mm thick. In a small bowl, mix together the parsley, Italian seasoning, oregano, olive oil, vinegar and pepper.

Set the Temperature to 325ºF/155ºC to allow the grill to preheat. Place the squash in the grill in overlapping slices and set the Timer to 6 minutes. When the Timer beeps, check the squash with the tip of a knife. It will be tender-crisp when done.

In a serving bowl, lightly toss the squash with the Italian dressing and serve immediately.

SERVES 4.

NUTRITIONAL ANALYSIS: Calories: **73**   Total fat: **5g**   Saturated fat: **>1g**
% calories from fat: **61**   Carbohydrates: **6 g**   Protein: **1 g**   Cholesterol: **0 mg**   Sodium: **15 mg**

LOW CARB

Purple Onion & Sweet Red Peppers

Colorful and full of flavor!

2	**sweet red peppers**
1	**medium purple/red onion**
1 T./14 g.	**garlic, finely minced**
1 t./5 g.	**black pepper**
1 t./ 5 ml.	**lemon juice**

Clean the peppers and remove the seeds and inner fibers. Slice into rings 1⁄4-inch/ 6 mm thick. Remove the outer skin from the onion and slice into rings 1⁄4-inch/ 6 mm thick. In a medium bowl, toss the vegetables with the garlic, pepper and lemon juice.

Set the Temperature to 350ºF/170ºC to allow the grill to preheat. Layer the peppers and onion in the grill and set the Timer for 5 minutes. When the Timer beeps, check the vegetables with the tip of a knife. They will be tender-crisp when done. Serve immediately on a warmed platter.

SERVES 4.

NUTRITIONAL ANALYSIS: Calories: **29** Total fat: **0g** Saturated fat: **>1g**
% calories from fat: 5 Carbohydrates: **7 g** Protein: **>1 g** Cholesterol: **0 mg** Sodium: **>1 mg**

Sicilian Grilled Eggplant

Ripe tomatoes pair with eggplant/aubergine in this traditional Italian dish.

1	medium-sized eggplant/aubergine
1 t./5 g.	black pepper
1/2 t./2.5 g.	salt
8 oz./235 ml.	can tomato sauce
1/2 c./115 g.	fresh ripe tomato, diced
1 T./14 g.	fresh garlic, minced
1 T./14 g.	fresh parsley, minced
1 t./5 g.	black pepper
1/2 t./2.5 g.	salt
2 T./28 g.	Asiago cheese/soft melting cheese, shredded

Clean, peel and cut the eggplant/aubergine into 1/2-inch/12-mm thick slices. Arrange the eggplant/aubergine slices on a double-thickness of paper towels and sprinkle with salt. Let stand 10 minutes. Rinse the salt away and pat dry. Sprinkle each slice with pepper. In a small saucepan, combine the tomato sauce, tomato, garlic, parsley, pepper and salt. Heat through and simmer for 10 minutes. Keep warm.

Set the Temperature to 350ºF/170ºC to allow the grill to preheat. Place the eggplant/aubergine slices in the grill in a single layer and set the Timer to 8 minutes. When the Timer beeps, check the eggplant/aubergine for tenderness.

Place on a large serving platter and grill any remaining slices as directed above. When all the eggplant/aubergine slices are grilled, gently pour the tomato sauce over the slices and top with the shredded cheese. **SERVES 4.**

NUTRITIONAL ANALYSIS: Calories: **77**   Total fat: **1g**   Saturated fat: **>1g**   % calories from fat: **15**   Carbohydrates: **15 g**   Protein: **3 g**   Cholesterol: **3 mg**   Sodium: **650 mg**

Asparagus with Lemon Dill Butter

Serve warm or, during the hottest days of summertime, chilled. Either way, it's delectable!

1 lb./450 g.	fresh asparagus
1/3 c./75 g.	lowfat margarine
2 t./10 ml.	lemon juice
1 t./5 g.	fresh dill, finely minced
1/4 t./1 g.	salt
1/4 t./1 g.	white pepper

Clean the asparagus and cut off the woody end pieces, if necessary, to fit inside the grill. Pat dry. In a small serving bowl, combine the margarine, lemon juice and dill.

Set the Temperature to 350ºF/170ºC and allow the grill to preheat. Place the asparagus side-by-side in the grill lengthwise (vertically) and lightly salt and pepper. Set the Timer for 3 minutes. When the Timer beeps, the asparagus should be tender-crisp. If not, grill for an additional 1 to 2 minutes. Be careful not to burn or overcook the asparagus.

Place the grilled asparagus on a warmed serving platter. To serve, place a tablespoon of the lemon butter on each serving of asparagus.

SERVES 4.

LOW CARB

NUTRITIONAL ANALYSIS: Calories: **65**   Total fat: **2g**   Saturated fat: **>1g**
% calories from fat: **35**   Carbohydrates: **6 g**   Protein: **2 g**   Cholesterol: **0 mg**   Sodium: **247 mg**

Tuscan Purple Onions

Perfect with beef or pork.

2 T./30 ml.	**extra virgin olive oil**
1 T./15 ml.	**balsamic vinegar**
1 t./5 g.	**fresh rosemary, finely minced**
2 T./28 g.	**fresh parsley, finely minced**
1/2 t./2.5 g.	**dried oregano**
1 t./5 g.	**black pepper**
1/4 t./1 g.	**salt**
1 lb./450 g.	**purple/red onions**

In a 9-inch x 13-inch/ 23 cm x 33 cm glass dish, combine the oil, vinegar, rosemary, parsley, oregano, pepper and salt. Cut the onions into slices 1⁄4-inch/6-mm thick. Do not separate the slices. Place each slice in the glass pan and turn to coat.

Set the Temperature to 350ºF/170ºC to allow the grill to preheat. Place the onion slices in a single layer on the grill. Close the grill and set the Timer to 5 minutes. When the Timer beeps, the onions should be tender-crisp. If not, continue grilling for 1 minute. Transfer the grilled onions to a serving platter and grill any remaining slices.

SERVES 6.

NUTRITIONAL ANALYSIS: Calories: **42** Total fat: **1g** Saturated fat: **>1g**
% calories from fat: **26** Carbohydrates: **7 g** Protein: **>1 g** Cholesterol: **0 mg** Sodium: **101 mg**

LOW CARB

Easy Barbequed Onions

Fast enough for any night of the week.

2	large sweet Vidalia/mild onions
1/4 c./60 ml.	prepared barbeque sauce
1/4 t./1 g.	black pepper
1/4 t./1 ml.	bottled hot sauce

Remove the outer skins from the onions and trim off the ends. Slice each onion into 1/4-inch/6-mm thick slices. Do not separate the slices. Combine the barbeque sauce, pepper and hot sauce in a small bowl.

Set the Temperature to 350ºF/170ºC to allow the grill to preheat. Place the onion slices in the grill and smooth 1 teaspoon/ 5 ml of sauce over each. Close the grill and set the Timer to 5 minutes. When the Timer beeps, the onions should be tender–crisp. If not, continue grilling for 1 to 2 minutes. Remove the onions from the grill and repeat the process with the remaining onions.

SERVES 4.

LOW CARB

NUTRITIONAL ANALYSIS: Calories: **46**   Total fat: **>1g**   Saturated fat: **>1g**
% calories from fat: **2**   Carbohydrates: **10 g**   Protein: **>1 g**   Cholesterol: **0 mg**   Sodium: **228 mg**

Mixed Vegetable Grill

The grilling process brings out the bold flavors of these vegetables.
Serve with a simple cut of chicken or beef.

1	red pepper, seeded
1	green pepper, seeded
1	small purple/red onion, peeled
1	medium zucchini/courgette squash, cleaned
1	carrot, peeled
2 T./30 ml.	extra virgin olive oil
1 T./15 ml.	lemon juice
1 t./5 g.	black pepper
1/2 t./2.5 g.	salt

Chop the peppers, onion, squash/courgette and carrot into 1/2-inch/12-mm pieces. In a small bowl, combine the oil, lemon juice, pepper and salt.

Set the Temperature to 350ºF/170ºC to allow the grill to preheat. Place the vegetables in the grill in an even layer and sprinkle with the oil and lemon seasonings. Set the Timer for 5 minutes. When the Timer beeps, the vegetables should be tender-crisp. If not, continue grilling for 1 to 2 minutes.

SERVES 4.

NUTRITIONAL   ANALYSIS: Calories: **54**   Total fat: **2g**   Saturated fat: **>1g**
% calories from fat: **30**   Carbohydrates: **9 g**   Protein: **2 g**   Cholesterol: **0 mg**   Sodium: **300 mg**

LOW CARB

Greek Vegetables with Lemon & Garlic

A subtle reminder of sun-drenched Greek Islands.

1 c./225 g.	**eggplant/aubergine cubes, 1/2-inch**/12-mm **each**
1	**red pepper, seeded, chopped**
1	**green pepper, seeded, chopped**
1	**small white onion, sliced thinly**
10	**button mushrooms, sliced**
2	**cloves garlic, finely minced**
2 T./30 ml.	**extra virgin olive oil**
1 T./15 ml.	**lemon juice**
1	**small tomato, chopped**
1	**small cucumber, peeled and chopped**

Set the Temperature to 350ºF/170ºC to allow the grill to preheat. Place the eggplant/aubergine, peppers and onion in the grill in an even layer and set the Timer for 3 minutes. When the Timer beeps, add the mushrooms and garlic and sprinkle with the olive oil and lemon juice. Continue grilling for 5 minutes. Place the mixed vegetables in a serving bowl, top with the chopped tomato and cucumber, and mix lightly.

SERVES 4.

NUTRITIONAL ANALYSIS: Calories: **95**   Total fat: **2g**   Saturated fat: **>1g**   % calories from fat: **20**   Carbohydrates: **18 g**   Protein: **3 g**   Cholesterol: **0 mg**   Sodium: **9 mg**

Yukon Gold Potato Wedges

These potatoes are slightly sweet and partner well with chicken and turkey.

4	Yukon Gold Potatoes/new potatoes
1 t./5 g.	black pepper
1 t./5 g.	seasoned salt
1/2 t./2.5 g.	onion powder

Scrub the potatoes and remove any blemishes. Cut each potato into 12 small wedges and place in a plastic bag. Add the pepper, salt and onion powder and shake the bag to coat the potatoes.

Set the Temperature to 400ºF/200ºC to allow the grill to preheat. Place the potatoes in a single layer in the grill and set the Timer for 7 minutes. When the Timer beeps, check the potatoes. If the potatoes are not tender, continue grilling for 1 to 2 minutes. Repeat the process with any remaining wedges.

SERVES 4.

NUTRITIONAL ANALYSIS: Calories: **125**   Total fat: **>1g**   Saturated fat: **>1g**
% calories from fat: **1**   Carbohydrates: **23 g**   Protein: **2 g**   Cholesterol: **0 mg**   Sodium: **361 mg**

Spicy French Fries

A delicious, healthy treat!

2	**russet potatoes/baking potatoes**
1 T./15 ml.	**extra virgin olive oil**
1 t./5 ml.	**lemon juice**
1 t./5 g.	**black pepper**
1 t./5 g.	**seasoned salt**

Scrub the potatoes and remove any blemishes. Cut each potato into fries, about 1/2-inch/12-mm thick and 4 inches/10 cm in length. Sprinkle the oil and lemon juice over the fries and let stand for 5 minutes.

      Set the Temperature to 400ºF/200ºC to allow the grill to preheat. Place the potatoes in a single layer widthwise (horizontally) in the grill, sprinkle with the pepper and seasoned salt, and set the Timer for 7 minutes. When the Timer beeps, check the potatoes. If the potatoes are not tender, continue grilling for 1 to 2 minutes. Repeat with any remaining fries.

SERVES 4.

NUTRITIONAL ANALYSIS: Calories: **96**   Total fat: **2g**   Saturated fat: **>1g**
% calories from fat: **19**   Carbohydrates: **14 g**   Protein: **2 g**   Cholesterol: **0 mg**   Sodium: **1,041 mg**

Rosemary & Sage Potatoes

These potatoes are an elegant addition to any meal.

2	**large baking potatoes**
1 T./14 g.	**fresh rosemary, finely minced**
1 t./5 g.	**dried sage**
1 T./14 g.	**black pepper, coarsely ground**
1 t./5 g.	**salt**

Scrub the potatoes and remove any blemishes. Cut each potato into slices about 1/2-inch/12-mm thick. Pat dry.

Set the Temperature to 400ºF/200ºC to allow the grill to preheat. Place the slices in the grill in a single layer and sprinkle the rosemary, sage, pepper and salt on top. Set the Timer for 7 minutes. When the Timer beeps, check the potatoes. If the potatoes are not tender, continue grilling for 1 to 2 minutes. Repeat the process with any remaining slices.

SERVES 4.

NUTRITIONAL ANALYSIS: Calories: **116** Total fat: **>1g** Saturated fat: **>1g**
% calories from fat: **2** Carbohydrates: **27 g** Protein: **3 g** Cholesterol: **0 mg** Sodium: **590 mg**

Cheesy Grilled New Potatoes

A satisfying snack with a spinkle of cheese.

16	**small new potatoes**
1/4 c./55 g.	**green/spring onions, thinly sliced**
1 t./5 g.	**black pepper**
1 t./5 g.	**garlic salt**
2 T./28 g.	**lowfat cheddar cheese, shredded**

Clean the potatoes and cut into slices 1/4-inch/6 mm thick. Pat dry. Set the Temperature to 400°F/200°C and allow the grill to preheat. Place one half of the slices in the grill, add half of the onions, and sprinkle with pepper and salt. Close the grill and set the Timer for 7 minutes.

When the Timer beeps, place the grilled potatoes on a warmed serving tray and top with half of the cheese. Repeat the process with the remaining potato slices, onions, pepper, salt and cheese.

SERVES 4.

NUTRITIONAL ANALYSIS: Calories: **438**   Total fat: **>1g**   Saturated fat: **>1g**
% calories from fat: **1**   Carbohydrates: **94 g**   Protein: **10 g**   Cholesterol: **>1 mg**   Sodium: **505 mg**

Garlic-Stuffed Red Potatoes

Perfect for garlic lovers. Use as an accompaniment to beef steaks or pork chops.

4	**medium-sized red potatoes**
5	**cloves garlic, thinly sliced**
1 t./5 g.	**fresh oregano, minced**
2 T./28 g.	**fresh parsley, finely minced**
1 t./5 g.	**salt**
1/2 t./2.5 g.	**black pepper**

Peel the potatoes and cut each into 1/4-inch/6 mm thick slices. With the tip of a very sharp knife, create a pocket in each potato slice and insert 1 slice of garlic into each pocket.

Set the Temperature to 400ºF/200ºC and allow the grill to preheat. Place the slices in the grill and sprinkle with the oregano, parsley, salt and pepper. Set the Timer for 7 minutes. When the Timer beeps, check the potatoes with the tip of a knife. If the potatoes are not tender, continue grilling for 1 to 2 minutes or until tender.

SERVES 4.

NUTRITIONAL ANALYSIS: Calories: **151**   Total fat: **>1g**   Saturated fat: **>1g**   % calories from fat: **1**   Carbohydrates: **29 g**   Protein: **3 g**   Cholesterol: **0 mg**   Sodium: **612 mg**

Dijon Parsley Potatoes

Cut the potato slices with uniform thickness for even grilling.

3	**large baking potatoes**
4 T./60 ml.	**Dijon mustard**
2 T./28 g.	**green/spring onions, finely chopped**
1 T./14 g.	**parsley, finely minced**
1 t./5 g.	**black pepper**

Clean the potatoes and cut each into 1⁄4-inch/6 mm thick cubes. Set the Temperature to 400ºF/200ºC and allow the grill to preheat. Place the potatoes in the grill in an even layer and lightly coat with Dijon mustard. Sprinkle with the onions, parsley and pepper.

Close the grill and set the Timer to 7 minutes. When the Timer beeps, check the potatoes with a tip of a knife. If they are not tender, continue grilling for 1 to 2 minutes.

SERVES 4.

NUTRITIONAL ANALYSIS: Calories: **159** Total fat: **3g** Saturated fat: **>1g** % calories from fat: **19** Carbohydrates: **27 g** Protein: **3 g** Cholesterol: **0 mg** Sodium: **306 mg**

Grilled Red Potato Hash

For lunch, dinner or a hearty snack.

2	**chicken breast halves, boned and skinned**
3	**large red potatoes**
1/2 c./115 g.	**white onion, chopped**
2 T./28 g.	**lowfat margarine**
1 t./5 g.	**seasoned salt**
1/2 t./2.5 g.	**black pepper**
2 T./28 g.	**fresh parsley, minced**

Set the Temperature to 375°F/185°C and allow the grill to preheat. Place the chicken in the grill and set the Timer to 5 minutes. When the Timer beeps, check the chicken with the tip of a knife. If the chicken is not cooked completely through, continue grilling for 1 to 2 minutes. Chop the chicken into small pieces and set aside.

Clean the potatoes and chop into small cubes (about 1/4-inch/6 mm). Set the Temperature to 400°F/200°C and add the potato cubes. Close the grill and set the Timer for 4 minutes.

In a small bowl, mix the margarine, salt and pepper with the onion and cooked chicken. Add the chicken and onion mixture to the potatoes in the grill. Spread evenly across the grill. Set the Timer for 4 minutes. When the Timer beeps, remove the hash to a serving platter. Garnish with the parsley and serve.

SERVES 4.

NUTRITIONAL ANALYSIS: Calories: **172**   Total fat: **2g**   Saturated fat: **>1g**
% calories from fat: **10**   Carbohydrates: **23 g**   Protein: **9 g**   Cholesterol: **18 mg**   Sodium: **639 mg**

Honey Butter Sweet Potatoes

Serve with grilled ham or pork chops.

3	medium sweet potatoes
1/2 c./115 g.	lowfat margarine
2 T./28 g.	clover honey
1/2 t./2.5 g.	ground cinnamon

Clean the potatoes, peel and cut into slices about 1/4-inch/6 mm thick. In a small bowl, combine the margarine, honey and cinnamon and stir until smooth.

Set the Temperature to 400ºF/200ºC to allow the grill to preheat. Place the potato slices in the grill and set the Timer for 3 minutes. When the Timer beeps, spoon the honey butter over the potatoes and set the Timer for 4 minutes. As the butter melts, it will run into the drip tray. Place the grilled potatoes on a serving platter and drizzle with the melted honey butter.

SERVES 4.

NUTRITIONAL ANALYSIS: Calories: **154**   Total fat: **3g**   Saturated fat: **1g**   % calories from fat: **20**   Carbohydrates: **27 g**   Protein: **1 g**   Cholesterol: **0 mg**   Sodium: **294 mg**

FRUIT & DESSERTS
Grilled Cinnamon Peaches & Papaya

The lightly grilled fruit is perfect for a warm summer evening.

3	**ripe peaches**
1	**ripe papaya**
1/4 c./55 g.	**lowfat margarine**
1/2 t./2.5 g.	**ground cinnamon**
1 T./15 ml.	**concentrated apple juice**

Pit and peel the peaches. Chop the fruit into small cubes (about 1/4-inch/6 mm thick). Peel and clean the papaya, remove the seeds, and chop into small cubes. In a medium bowl, combine the margarine, cinnamon and apple juice and blend well. Add the peaches and papaya and toss lightly.

Set the Temperature to 300ºF/140ºC and allow the grill to preheat. Place the fruit in an even layer in the grill and set the Timer for 2 minutes. When the Timer beeps, check the fruit with the tip of a knife. The fruit will be warm and lightly glazed when done.

SERVES 4.

NUTRITIONAL ANALYSIS: Calories: **94**   Total fat: **2g**   Saturated fat: **>1g**
% calories from fat: **16**   Carbohydrates: **18 g**   Protein: **1 g**   Cholesterol: **0 mg**   Sodium: **79 mg**

Grilled Apple Pecan Cups

Crunchy pecans naturally accompany sweet and crisp apples.

2	small baking apples
1/4 c./55 g.	clover honey
2 T./28 g.	pecans, chopped
1 T./14 g.	brown sugar

Peel, core and cut the apples in half crosswise. Inside the "cup" of each half, place a tablespoon/14 g. of honey. Sprinkle 1 teaspoon/5 ml. of the chopped pecans into each "cup" of honey and dust the apples with the brown sugar.

Set the Temperature to 300°F/140°C and allow the grill to preheat. Place the apples, cut side up, in the grill and set the Timer for 3 minutes. Watch carefully as the apples grill to avoid burning. When the Timer beeps, check the apples with the tip of a knife to make sure they are tender. If not, continue grilling for 1 to 2 minutes. When done, top each apple with frozen lowfat vanilla yogurt, if desired.

SERVES 4.

NUTRITIONAL ANALYSIS: Calories: **157** Total fat: **3g** Saturated fat: **>1g** % calories from fat: **17** Carbohydrates: **29 g** Protein: **>1 g** Cholesterol: **0 mg** Sodium: **1 mg**

Hawaiian Pineapple Slices

This is so versatile—serve as a salad or a dessert!

1	fresh pineapple
1/4 c./55 g.	clover honey
1 t./5 g.	ground cinnamon

Peel, core and slice the pineapple into 1/2-inch/12 mm thick slices. In a small bowl, combine the honey and cinnamon.

Set the Temperature to 300°F/140°C and allow the grill to preheat. Place the slices in a single layer in the grill and drizzle the honey-cinnamon over the slices. Close the grill and set the Timer to 3 minutes, or until the pineapple is tender. Repeat with any remaining slices.

SERVES 6.

NUTRITIONAL ANALYSIS: Calories: **83** Total fat: **>1g** Saturated fat: **>1g**
% calories from fat: **3** Carbohydrates: **22 g** Protein: **>1 g** Cholesterol: **0 mg** Sodium: **1 mg**

Quick & Easy Grilled Bananas

This is just about the easiest fruit dessert you'll find.

2	ripe bananas, peeled
2 T./28 g.	sugar
1/2 t./2.5 g.	ground cinnamon
2 T./28 g.	walnuts, finely minced

Cut the bananas in half widthwise and in half lengthwise. Combine the sugar, cinnamon and walnuts in a small bowl.

Set the Temperature to 300ºF/140ºC to allow the grill to preheat. Place the bananas in the grill widthwise (horizontally) and spoon the cinnamon-walnuts over each slice. Set the Timer for 3 minutes. When the Timer beeps, check the fruit. The bananas will be warm and the cinnamon-walnuts slightly glazed when done.

SERVES 2.

NUTRITIONAL ANALYSIS: Calories: **262**   Total fat: **5g**   Saturated fat: **>1g**
% calories from fat: **18**   Carbohydrates: **44 g**   Protein: **2 g**   Cholesterol: **0 mg**   Sodium: **13 mg**

Grilled Strawberry Maple Shortcake

Friends popping in? Try this for a quick-fix dessert.

1	**lowfat pound/madeira cake, cut into 8 slices**
1/4 c./60 ml.	**maple syrup**
2 c./450 g.	**fresh strawberries, cleaned and sliced**
1 c./235 ml.	**nonfat whipped cream topping**

Set the Temperature to 325ºF/155ºC and allow the grill to preheat. Place the cake slices evenly in the grill and brush with the maple syrup. Close the grill and set the Timer for 3 minutes. When done, the cake will be toasted and completely warm. To serve, place the cake slices on individual plates, top with strawberries and cover with whipped topping.

SERVES 4.

NUTRITIONAL ANALYSIS: Calories: **460**   Total fat: **3g**   Saturated fat: **>1g**   % calories from fat: **7**   Carbohydrates: **82 g**   Protein: **6 g**   Cholesterol: **0 mg**   Sodium: **319 mg**

SALADS
Asian Noodle Steak Salad

Serve warm or cold for a delicious, satisfying meal.

1/2 lb./225 g.	lean beef steak
1	red pepper, seeded and thinly sliced
1 c./225 g.	fresh bean sprouts
8 oz./225 g.	vermicelli pasta, cooked and drained
1/4 c./60 ml.	low sodium soy sauce
1 t./5 g.	black pepper
1/2 t./2.5 g.	ground ginger
1	clove garlic, minced
1 t./5 g.	brown sugar
1/2 t./2.5 ml.	Asian chile oil
3 oz./85 g.	dry roasted peanuts, coarsely chopped

Remove all visible fat from the beef. Cut the beef into very thin slices. Set the Temperature to 400°F/200°C to allow the grill to preheat. Set the Timer to 2 minutes for medium-rare beef, or continue grilling if desired.

In a large serving bowl, combine the beef, red pepper, bean sprouts and pasta. In a small bowl, prepare the salad dressing by combining the soy sauce, black pepper, ginger, garlic, brown sugar and chile oil. Pour the dressing over the salad and toss all the ingredients together. Top with the chopped peanuts.

SERVES 6.

NUTRITIONAL ANALYSIS: Calories: **217**   Total fat: **11g**   Saturated fat: **2g**
% calories from fat: **43**   Carbohydrates: **18 g**   Protein: **15 g**   Cholesterol: **23 mg**   Sodium: **708 mg**

Garden Vegetable Fettuccini Salad

Balsamic vinegar, oil and garlic accentuate the vegetables perfectly.

1	red pepper, cut into 1-inch/2.5 cm pieces
1	green pepper, cut into 1-inch/2.5 cm pieces
2 c./450 g.	eggplant/aubergine, cut into 1/2-inch/2 mm pieces
1/2 c./115 g.	white onion, cut into 1-inch/2.5 cm pieces
1	clove garlic, finely minced
1	ripe tomato, chopped
8 oz./225 g.	fettuccini noodles, cooked
1 T./15 ml.	roasted garlic-flavored oil
2 T./30 ml.	balsamic vinegar
1 t./5 g.	dried Italian seasoning
1 T./14 g.	fresh parsley, minced
1/2 t./2.5 g.	salt
1/2 t./2.5 g.	dried rosemary
1 t./5 g.	coarsely ground black pepper

Set the Temperature to 350°F/170°C and allow the grill to preheat. Place the peppers, eggplant/aubergine, onion and garlic in the grill and set the Timer for 6 minutes. When the Timer beeps, remove the vegetables and cool slightly.

In a large serving bowl, combine the grilled vegetables, chopped tomato and fettuccini noodles. Mix together the oil, vinegar, Italian seasoning, parsley, salt, rosemary and black pepper to make the salad dressing. Pour the dressing over the salad and toss gently to blend the flavors. **SERVES 6.**

NUTRITIONAL ANALYSIS: Calories: **93** Total fat: **3g** Saturated fat: **>1g**
% calories from fat: **26** Carbohydrates: **15 g** Protein: **3 g** Cholesterol: **12 mg** Sodium: **14 mg**

Summer Berry Salad

Pair this salad with Sage-Stuffed Chicken Breasts (p. 131), for a perfect summer evening meal!

2 c./450 g.	**fresh strawberries, cleaned and cut in halves**
1 c./225 g.	**fresh raspberries, cleaned**
1/2 c./115 g.	**fresh blueberries**
1	**peach, peeled, pitted and sliced**
1/2 c./120 ml.	**nonfat sour cream**
1 t./5 g.	**sugar**
1 T./15 ml.	**lemon juice**

In a large salad bowl, combine the fruit. Mix together the sour cream, sugar and lemon juice in a small bowl and drizzle over the fruit. Toss lightly and serve at once.

SERVES 4.

NUTRITIONAL ANALYSIS: Calories: **89**   Total fat: **>1g**   Saturated fat: **>1g**   % calories from fat: **5**   Carbohydrates: **20 g**   Protein: **3 g**   Cholesterol: **0 mg**   Sodium: **32 mg**

Grilled Chicken Fruit Salad

Substitute turkey or lean pork, if desired.

1	chicken breast half, skinned and boned
2 c./450 g.	seedless red grapes, halved
1/2 c./115 g.	celery, chopped
1/4 c./55 g.	white onion, chopped
2 T./28 g.	walnuts, finely chopped
1/2 c./120 ml.	nonfat mayonnaise
1 T./15 ml.	Dijon mustard
1/2 t./2.5 g.	salt
1/2 t./2.5 g.	black pepper
1 T./15 ml.	lemon juice

Set the Temperature to 375ºF/185ºC and allow the grill to preheat. Place the chicken in the grill and set the Timer to 5 minutes. When the Timer beeps, check the chicken with the tip of a knife. If the chicken is not cooked completely through, continue grilling for 1 to 2 minutes. Chop the chicken into small pieces and set aside.

In a large salad bowl, combine the chicken, grapes, celery, onion and walnuts. Mix together the mayonnaise, mustard, salt, pepper and juice to make a dressing. Pour over the chicken salad and toss lightly.

SERVES 4.

NUTRITIONAL ANALYSIS: Calories: **222**   Total fat: **5g**   Saturated fat: **>1g**   % calories from fat: **21**   Carbohydrates: **24 g**   Protein: **15 g**   Cholesterol: **37 mg**   Sodium: **671 mg**

Green Garden Salad with Herb & Bacon Vinaigrette

This appetizing salad with good textures can accompany almost any chop or steak.

4 c./900 g.	torn dark green lettuce leaves
1/2 c./115 g.	celery, sliced
4	radishes, sliced
1/2 c./115 g.	frozen peas, thawed and drained
1	large tomato, cut into wedges
1/2	small purple/red onion, sliced and separated into rings
4	slices turkey bacon
2 T./30 ml.	extra virgin olive oil
2 T./30 ml.	balsamic vinegar
2 T./30 ml.	water
1 t./5 g.	garlic powder
1/2 t./2.5 g.	salt
1 t./5 g.	black pepper, coarsely ground

In a large salad bowl, combine the lettuce, celery, radishes, peas, tomato and onion. Refrigerate. Set the Temperature to 400ºF/200ºC to allow the grill to preheat. Place the bacon slices in the grill and set the Timer to 3 minutes. When the Timer beeps, remove the bacon and cool. Crumble and set aside.

Assemble the dressing by blending the oil, vinegar, water, garlic powder, salt and pepper. Shake well. Pour the dressing over the salad, toss the ingredients and garnish with the bacon. **SERVES 4.**

NUTRITIONAL ANALYSIS:	Calories: **195**	Total fat: **9g**	Saturated fat: **1g**
% calories from fat: **49**	Carbohydrates: **16 g**	Protein: **6 g**	Cholesterol: **13 mg**	Sodium: **538 mg**

Grilled Vegetable Pasta Salad

Fresh vegetables and tender pasta make a beautiful presentation!

2	zucchini/courgettes, thinly sliced
1	small purple/red onion, thinly sliced
1	clove garlic, finely minced
1	red pepper, chopped
8 oz./225 g.	linguine pasta, cooked
1 T./15 ml.	balsamic vinegar
2 T./30 ml.	extra virgin olive oil
1 t./5 g.	black pepper
1/2 t./2.5 g.	ground oregano
2 T./28 g.	Italian parsley, chopped
1/2 t./2.5 g.	salt
1	ripe tomato, chopped

Set the Temperature to 350ºF/170ºC and allow the grill to preheat. Place the zucchini/courgettes, onion, garlic and red pepper in the grill in even layers and set the Timer for 6 minutes. When the Timer beeps, remove the vegetables and cool.

In a large serving bowl, combine the grilled vegetables and cooked linguine. In a small bowl, combine the vinegar, oil, black pepper, oregano, Italian parsley and salt to make the dressing. Pour the dressing over the linguine and vegetables, toss and garnish with the chopped tomato. **SERVES 4.**

NUTRITIONAL ANALYSIS: Calories: **172**   Total fat: **8g**   Saturated fat: **1g**
% calories from fat: **39**   Carbohydrates: **22 g**   Protein: **5 g**   Cholesterol: **19 mg**   Sodium: **302 mg**

THE GEORGE FOREMAN® LEAN MEAN FAT REDUCING GRILLING MACHINE
Basic Cooking Guide

To adapt your recipes to *The George Foreman® Lean Mean Fat Reducing Grilling Machine* and to create new ones, we suggest you start with the basic cooking guide that follows. Food is very rarely perfectly uniform in size so you'll find that some of the suggested times will need to be adjusted to your foods as they grill. We've included the following tips that will help you enjoy the full range of features offered by your *George Foreman® Lean Mean Fat Reducing Grilling Machine*:

■ Carefully read the Owner's Manual that accompanies your grill. The grill is an easy and carefree appliance when used and cleaned properly.

■ Use the plastic spatula to remove foods from the grill or to clean debris from the grilling plates.

■ Some foods cook more uniformly when placed horizontally or vertically in the grill. For example, asparagus should be placed lengthwise (vertically) across the grill. Most kebabs grill best widthwise (horizontally) across the grill. If you aren't sure which way is best, try one direction for about 1–2 minutes and then check the food. Rearrange food as needed.

■ An uneven cut of meat or a chop may display "char marks" on one side as it grills. Although this does not have any effect on the results of the grilled foods, you may rearrange the meat to "even out" the marks, if you desire. You do not have to turn meat over while it grills because the grill cooks both sides at the same time, however you may turn meat if you want to baste it or reposition it.

■ We suggest you use a nonfat cooking spray in the grill prior to putting sticky or sweet foods into it. This is optional, but it helps to protect the nonstick grill surface and aids in removing the food after it grills.

The George Foreman® Lean Mean Fat Reducing Grilling Machine Basic Cooking Guide

Food	Temperature	Grilling Minutes	Notes
BEEF			
Flank steak/skirt steak	400°F/200°C	6–7	Slice thinly to serve
Hamburger, -4 oz./115 g.	350°F/170°C	4–5	
-8 oz./225 g.		5–6	
Kebabs	350°F/170°C	6–7	1-inch/2.5 cm pieces
London broil/hindquarter flank	400°F/200°C	6–7	1 1/2–2 inches/4-5 cm thick
Ribeye	400°F/200°C	5–7	
Ribs, -Short ribs	350°F/170°C	7–8	Parboil/steam prior to grilling
-Loin ribs	350°F/170°C	6–7	Parboil/steam prior to grilling
Round steak	400°F/200°C	3–4	
Sirloin	400°F/200°C	5–6	
T-Bone	400°F/200°C	5–6	
Tenderloin/filet	400°F/200°C	4–6	
FRUIT			
Apple	300°F/140°C	2–3	cut in half or sliced
Bananas	300°F/140°C	2–3	sliced lengthwise
Nectarines	300°F/140°C	2–3	cut in half or sliced
Peaches	300°F/140°C	2–3	cut in half or sliced
Pineapple	300°F/140°C	2–3	1/2-inch/12 mm thick slices
LAMB			
Ground lamb	350°F/170°C	6–7	
Kebabs	350°F/170°C	7–8	1-inch/2.5 cm pieces
Loin chops	350°F/170°C	4–6	
PORK			
Center cut chops	350°F/170°C	5–6	
Ground pork	350°F/170°C	7–8	

Food	Temperature	Grilling Minutes	Notes
PORK (continued)			
Ham	350°F/170°C	3–4	fully cooked, 1/2-inch/12 mm thick slice
Kebabs	350°F/170°C	7–8	1-inch/2.5 cm pieces
Loin chops	350°F/170°C	5–6	
Ribs, -Baby back ribs/rib			
part of loin chop	350°F/170°C	5–7	Parboil/steam prior to grilling
-Country-style ribs	350°F/170°C	8–10	boneless
Sausage	350°F/170°C	4–5	lowfat, link/banger or patty style
Tenderloin/filet	350°F/170°C	6–8	
POULTRY			
Chicken breasts	375°F/185°C	5–7	boneless/skinless
Chicken kebabs	350°F/170°C	7–8	1-inch/2.5 cm pieces
Chicken sausage	350°F/170°C	5–7	lowfat, link/banger or patty style
Chicken thighs	375°F/185°C	5–7	boneless/skinless
Ground chicken	350°F/170°C	5–7	
Ground turkey	350°F/170°C	7–8	
Turkey breast, -boneless/skinless			
-Thin sliced	350°F/170°C	3–4	
-Sliced		5–7	1/4–1/2 inch/6-12 mm thick
SANDWICHES			
Cheese	400°F/200°C	2–3	
Ham	400°F/200°C	5–6	
Roast Beef	400°F/200°C	2–3	
Rueben	400°F/200°C	2–3	
Sausage	400°F/200°C	2–3	
Turkey	400°F/200°C	2–3	
SEAFOOD			
Halibut steak	300°F/140°C	6–8	1/2–1 inch/12-25 mm thick
Kebabs	300°F/140°C	4–6	1–inch/25 mm pieces

Food	Temperature	Grilling Minutes	Notes
SEAFOOD (continued)			
Mahi Mahi fillet	300°F/140°C	3–5	
Orange Roughy fillet	300°F/140°C	4–6	
Red Snapper fillet	300°F/140°C	3–5	
Salmon, -Fillet	300°F/140°C	3–4	
-Steak		6–8	1/2–1 inch/12-25 mm thick
Scallops	300°F/140°C	3–4	
Sea Bass fillet	300°F/140°C	3–5	
Shrimp	300°F/140°C	1–2	
Swordfish steak	375°F/185°C	6–9	1/2–1 inch/12-25 mm thick
Tuna steak	375°F/185°C	4–6	1/2–1 inch/12-25 mm thick
SNACKS			
Calzone	350°F/170°C	8–9	
Hot Dogs	400°F/200°C	2–3	
Quesadillas	400°F/200°C	2–3	
Tacos	375°F/185°C	6–8	meat filling
VEGETABLES			
Asparagus	350°F/170°C	3–4	lengthwise (vertically) on grill
Brussels sprouts	350°F/170°C	8–9	frozen, thawed
Carrots	350°F/170°C	5–7	1/4–1/2 inch/6-12 mm thick slices
Eggplant/aubergine	350°F/170°C	8–9	1/4–1/2 inch/6-12 mm thick slices or cubed
Mushrooms	350°F/170°C	5–6	portabellas or other thick-cut mushrooms
Onions	350°F/170°C	5–6	thinly sliced
Peppers	350°F/170°C	6–8	thinly sliced
Potatoes, -Baking	400°F/200°C	7–9	1/4–1/2 inch/6-12 mm thick slices
-cubed Red		7–9	1/4–1/2 inch/6-12 mm thick slices
-cubed Sweet		7–9	1/4–1/2 inch/6-12 mm thick slices
Squash	325°F/155°C	6–8	1/4–1/2 inch/6-12 mm thick slices or cubed

INDEX